THEY CALL ME
OIL CAN

BASEBALL, DRUGS,
and LIFE ON THE EDGE

Dennis "Oil Can" Boyd
with Mike Shalin

TRIUMPH
B O O K S

Library of Congress Cataloging-in-Publication Data

Boyd, Dennis, 1959-
    They call me Oil Can : baseball, drugs, and life on the edge / Dennis "Oil Can" Boyd with Mike Shalin.
        p. cm.
    ISBN 978-1-60078-682-2 (hardback)
1. Boyd, Dennis, 1959-2. Baseball players—United States—Biography. 3. Pitchers (Baseball)—United States—Biography.
I. Shalin, Mike, 1954- II. Title.
    GV865.B698A3 2012
    796.357092—dc23
    [B]   2012001198

This book is available in quantity at special discounts for your group or organization. For further information, contact:

Triumph Books LLC
542 South Dearborn Street
Suite 750
Chicago, Illinois 60605
(312) 939-3330
Fax (312) 663-3557
www.triumphbooks.com

Printed in U.S.A.

ISBN: 978-1-60078-682-2

Design by Sue Knopf

Photos courtesy of Dennis Boyd except where otherwise noted.

For my family: Karen, Dennis II, and Tala

—Oil Can

To Mary, my significantly better half,
and to my boys—Josh, Taylor, and Mac.
You four are the reason for everything!

To my brothers, who taught me
anything about sports worth knowing.

To Mom and Dad—
you are both gone but never forgotten.

To Sheila, for being a friend
through these many, many, many, many years.

To Ted Baxter—
you will always be an inspiration.

And to Oil Can—
I'm proud to have done this together!

—Mike Shalin

"In 1985, the *Globe* sent me to Meridian, Mississippi, to do a story on Dennis 'Oil Can' Boyd's background. I had dinner with his father, Willie James, who was once a Negro League pitcher and maintained the field and team in Meridian. He was telling me how he financed his life in baseball by being a landscaper.

"He told me a story of a day in 1964 when he was landscaping the yard of the grand dragon of the Ku Klux Klan. He remembered seeing the cars coming up. They all rolled up the street, up the road from Philadelphia to Mississippi to take care of some civil rights workers.

"Mr. Boyd looked me in the eye. He said, 'You know what? This is what makes this country great. Today that man is destitute and crippled with arthritis, and my boy, Dennis Boyd, is pitching in the major leagues for the Boston Red Sox.'

"In my mind the Boyd family represents baseball's place in American society."

—*Peter Gammons,*
in his Hall of Fame speech, 2005

Contents

Foreword

My relationship with Can was a pitcher/catcher relationship. What I loved about him was that the guy could pitch. He had a good idea what he wanted; he had great instincts, touch, and feel for his pitches; and he had great weapons to get people out. He thinks like a champion. He saw stuff that a lot of people didn't. He saw swings coming through the zone and he knew when to throw a change-up and when to throw a breaking ball, when to mix in a fastball, when to cut a pitch. He could slow a guy's bat down or speed it up—all the planning in his own head. It's a beautiful picture when you do that stuff.

That's the way I saw him pitch; and he had great confidence. My job was just to make sure to keep him focused. It really wasn't that hard to do. You just had to kind of remind him how to channel his energy.

Because of that, we had a wonderful relationship. He knew that I cared about him and I cared about the team and I was going to help him to do what he wanted to do, which was find a way to win.

He called his own pitches. That's fine. Pitchers—that's the way they think. He did what he wanted to do. He could live with it. He was a man. He knew himself. He knew his strengths and weaknesses. The only thing that I tried to do was make sure he didn't get distracted. I think sometimes he got to an edge, he went a little overboard, and my job was to keep it at the right level. I think we did that well together.

I'd say, "Well, what do you want to do here?" And he'd come right out with it. I didn't disagree, because I believed that if you're 100 percent sticking with what you want to do and you believe in it, it's going to work, somehow. And not only that, but if it doesn't work you can live with it and you can learn from it.

He didn't have many doubts when he was out there throwing a baseball, I can tell you that!

Off the field, I never had a problem with Can. It took a while to get to know each other, respect each other, earn each other's respect. It's not like we went out partying or whatever. I didn't see him much away from the field and when I did see him I'd say hello. We were very cordial to each other. He became a good teammate. I'd do anything for him that I could. I think that's the way we all were about each other.

I still see him from time to time at functions. I think the game of baseball, it's something that you get to do, and the times that you get to play games and have some success together are times you don't forget. They're your most trying times. There were times when things didn't work and you're very vulnerable and you needed somebody to be there with you and for you, and I think we were there for each other. When he had success, so did I. When he failed, I failed with him. That's the way it goes.

You want to know how competitive Oil Can was? Look at Eddie Murray. Oil Can frustrated Eddie Murray. Murray was a Hall of Famer and I think he might have hit one home run off of Can—and when he did it took him two minutes to get around the bases. It was obvious that Can frustrated him.

Can was excitable on the mound. He was very passionate about what he did—especially if he got a big out in a big situation, he didn't hide the way he felt about it. With that, you create some enemies who want to beat you. Not that we didn't want to beat each other as it was, but sometimes when you get a little excessive, or a little excited, people don't like that stuff. All in all, though, I think he was well respected by his opposition and his teammates on the field.

If I had to sum up Oil Can Boyd in one word, it would be "special." That's the way I see him!

— *Rich Gedman, former Red Sox catcher*

Author's Note

My name is Dennis Boyd. They call me "Oil Can." I'd like to introduce you to my life, and I'd like to tell you about my journey to—and in and after—the major leagues. I would like to show you my colorful background and the folklore of my life. This will be a great, great adventure. Sit back, enjoy, and take a ride—'cause this is a great story about a baseball player who has had a wonderful life and comes from a great background in baseball and society.

I spend a lot of time these days doing charity events for the Boston Red Sox, doing card shows, and doing fantasy camps, and one thing is abundantly clear to me: love me or hate me, people will never forget Oil Can Boyd.

Life has been a great experience for me. Baseball has taken me on a super journey and, in a round-about way I'm ending up as I began—loving the game of baseball.

Some of the things in the book you're about to read will make you smile. Some of the things you read will shock you. Some of the language in this book is a little explicit. But just hang in and go along for the ride. I think you'll enjoy it.

—*The Can, 2011*

Prologue: October 1986

McNamara said, "Can, man, we're going to go with Bruce tomorrow night."

"What do you mean, Skip? Are you telling me that I'm not going to pitch tomorrow night?"

"Don't get upset," he said, "it's a strategic move."

"Strategic?"

"The reason we're going with Bruce is because of the rain delay." Then he said that Bruce Hurst pitched well against the Mets the first two games.

"Skip," I said, "I had an extra day of rest. I'm ready to go."

After starting to cry, I turned and went upstairs. My friend, Gary Finizio, was staying at the hotel as my guest. He'd been out to dinner with my wife and me, at Rusty Staub's, before I'd met with McNamara. I went to his room and he saw I was upset and said, "What's wrong?"

"They ain't letting me pitch."

"What you mean they won't let pitch?"

I told him I had to get out and he said he was going with me. I went back downstairs, where a lot of my teammates were either in the lobby or in the bar having a drink, and left the hotel with

1

Gary. My friend and teammate, Al Nipper, tried to stop me. He could see I was crying and he knew where I was heading. He tried to hold me back. He teared up himself.

I told him not to follow me. He knew where I was going and I didn't want him to see.

I was walking toward Central Park, crying as I walked. When I got to where I knew I had to be, I told Gary to wait and I made a deal, while crying, talking to the dope dealer.

I got the dope and headed back to the hotel, got back to my room, and started to get high. I stayed up all night; couldn't get to sleep. The more hurt I felt, the more cocaine I wanted to do.

All the while I'm saying to myself, "Why me? Why now?" *Goddamn* I wanted to pitch!

Twenty-five years later, John McNamara said I was too drunk to pitch in Game 7. Twenty-five years later, I guess that's how John McNamara felt, but there's no evidence of that ever happening, because it *didn't* happen. Mind you, this is Game 7, man. C'mon, be real. I was told the day of the rainout that I wasn't pitching and I did what I did on that day. But I still had to go to bed and get ready to play in Game 7, because at the same time I was told that I wasn't starting Game 7 I was told I'd be the first pitcher up if Bruce got in any trouble.

Now, that did make me feel a little bit better, I admit—even though I walked out and walked up the street to buy cocaine. But this was Game 7. It's a night ballgame. I got to the ballpark somewhere around 2:00 or 2:30 in the afternoon on the bus. The wives and everything would come later, but my wife was there the whole time, so she was quite disturbed that McNamara would say that I wasn't prepared to pitch.

The whole damn season was a roller coaster ride for me, and this could've been the redemption. I think that nobody wanted to eat crow. They knew, all of them—the media, the administration

2

of the Red Sox, even Major League Baseball—what this could mean. When I walked out because I didn't get picked for the All-Star Game—which I felt I should have been picked for and possibly could have started—that'd been the low point, but now that redemption was possible I think that nobody wanted to eat the crow that they knew would come with me winning Game 7 of the World Series.

All the pitchers were down in the bullpen when Bruce was warming up. We'd had batting practice and everything, we'd gone in and got ready to play the ballgame. So where am I supposed to be drunk at? We got batting practice before the game—I think that's a regimen that's been going for 100 years—you get out there and get loose, all the stuff you do. You shag yourself some fly balls, do what you have to do to get ready for a game. So where am I supposed to be drunk at? You come into the clubhouse, you change into your uniform, and you get ready to go play a baseball game. You got 35 to 40 minutes after batting practice, and we're the last team to hit, because we're the visiting team. So where am I supposed to be getting drunk at?

They said Al Nipper told Bill Fischer I was drunk and he told McNamara. Nipper said they had to lock me in a room. I'll tell you right now, that's bullshit. It didn't happen. I talked to Al Nipper and I know that didn't happen. They're lying.

Nip said there was a meeting with McNamara, Fischer, Haywood Sullivan, and Lou Gorman and they called Nipper in and told him to check on me. He left the office and said, "I ain't fucking doing that."

I wasn't drunk; simple as that. McNamara's a liar. Now, I care for that man, but he's lying.

After the ball went through Bill Buckner's legs, I was getting ready to pitch the next day. That's all that was on my goddamn mind. So you ain't telling me I wasn't ready to pitch. My wife was in the room with me and she ain't ever known me not ready to pitch. John McNamara ain't ever known me to not be ready to pitch. For God sakes, the man said he's been managing baseball for a long time and I'm in the top five pitchers that he's ever seen. And he ain't going to put me on the mound? He made that comment. I didn't make that comment. And he ain't going to pitch me?

Charles Moss, the trainer, told me how he went to John McNamara and told him I wasn't prepared to pitch. It was on Charlie Moss to monitor me, follow me all around. It wasn't that he was with me, but I knew he was doing that shit and I knew people were reporting back to him. They had narcotics agents and all kinds of shit following me around the hotel, following me around New York City. I couldn't go shopping with my wife—they were outside my door, going down the elevator with me. Believe me, they're talking to me, they're telling me who they are. They ain't hiding nothing.

"Uhhhh, I was told to follow you." Some man told me that shit. Suit and tie. Very distinguished looking—kind of scary, actually. Everywhere I went in the city. We were walking around downtown and I told my wife, "We being followed." I knew this man was too close to me. I didn't lose him when I went to buy the cocaine; but they didn't want to bust me. I'm not a criminal. I'm a baseball player. Bottom line: I won 16 ballgames and missed a month. And the thing was, I won 16 games and half of them I don't even remember. Shit, and you're going to tell me I can't pitch?

These guys are out here healthy and winning 15 games, and I can throw my hat out on the field and win 15 games. Shit, I can throw a shoe out there and win 15 games. If I'm healthy, I'm winning 18, 19 games. I was never healthy and I won 78 games. I wasn't healthy my whole career and I'm still better than a .500 pitcher.

I was in the bullpen because I was told I was coming in. I was very ready—sitting on the bullpen bench, very anxious but upset. I know I should be out there and I know if I get out there I'm going to mow them down, because nobody beats me twice. That was my forte in the major leagues—if I faced a team back to back I never lost twice. I always made the adjustments.

I was in the bullpen, ready to pitch. I stayed there for five innings. Everybody was going in the game. I counted like five guys who pitched before me—even Al Nipper. I got so upset that I walked out of the bullpen into that tunnel in left field, lit a cigarette, started smoking it, and I started crying, walking back to the clubhouse. You had to go through the clubhouse before you got into the dugout. I came out into the dugout and watched us lose the World Series. I'm sitting there on the bench—and at the end of the game you can see me—and I'm crying.

If I'm crying how can people say I wasn't ready to pitch? If I cared that much, how can people say that?

For years I've been messed up about this—not taking anything away from my team because I thought we had the best team, but not without me pitching. We didn't put the best team on the field to beat the Mets in Game 7.

When we lost, I was crying in the clubhouse along with everyone else. Don Baylor came by me and rubbed me on the head. "I'm glad to see you grew up," he said to me. I wasn't sure how to take it at first, but eventually I took it as something about what he was seeing in me, that I was able to take the good with the bad, and I had done that.

Probably like most people, my entire life has been lived experiencing the good and the bad. What happened in New

York in '86, when the fates and then my manager took me out of my start in Game 7 of the World Series, was part of learning to live with the bad. But there has been a lot of good, right up until today, when at age 52 I can still go out onto the baseball field and play this game.

And I'm going to keep playing this game.

1: The Beginning

"I'm still tormented by my past
and it's hard to let go, because
you can't let go of blackness."

The Beginning

I'd like to begin back in 1964, in Mississippi. I was five years old—I turned six years old October 6, 1965, the same year I saw Martin Luther King in our church—but I can remember in the summer of '64, as a little-bitty boy, when these two white kids, Michael Schwerner and Andrew Goodman, and this black kid, James Chaney, came to Mississippi protesting for civil rights. They'd been all over country campaigning for civil rights, but then they came to the South, all the Southern states—Mississippi, Tennessee, Alabama, Georgia—and then they came to Meridian, Mississippi.

In the process of doing this they were murdered in '64, and their bodies were found two or three months later under a dam outside of Meridian, in a town called Williamsville, not too far from an Indian reservation.

At the time, we had my family—my dad, Willie Boyd Sr., better known as Skeeter; my mom, Girtharee Boyd, better known as Sweetie; and also one of my older brothers, Mike—at home. I was introduced to those three kids by my Uncle Frank, who brought them from the swimming pool in Meridian. At the time, there was segregation and we had a white swimming pool and a black swimming pool. He brought home James Chaney, the black guy, and the two white kids, who were from New York.

They were young men, I would imagine 20, 21, somewhere around there. I do remember quite well sitting in one of these white kids' lap and getting the comb caught in his hair. At the time, I didn't know what a cowlick was, or anything like that, but it was the part of the hair that was located in the middle of white kids' heads. So my mom had to cut the comb out of his hair.

After they got through visiting us they were supposed to leave and head up to Memphis. My Uncle Frank was in the car with them and my mom got him out of the car. She said, "Those boys ain't never going to be seen again and he ain't going nowhere." So Uncle Frank got out of the car, and then they left our house and they were picked up by the police and put in jail and kept there for a period of time.

At that time there was a curfew and after curfew nobody was on the streets. So, in other words: no witnesses. So they let the boys out of jail and told them to get on their way. And as they got going on out of town they were followed and intercepted about 25 miles outside of Meridian. A few months later they were found, up on the dam, buried, bodies crushed, covered up by bulldozers. Mangled and murdered by the Klan, but with the police's help. That's what made them stop. They saw sirens behind them—you're obeying the law and that's what's going to kill you.

I found out years later that these same kids who were at my house were murdered, and their story was made into the movie *Mississippi Burning*. That's why today, what I've gone through, I don't trust the police. Not in the South, not *nowhere*. I'm sorry.

The first white person who ever touched me was those two white kids. They were the first white people who ever came in my house. And the Ku Klux Klan murdered those kids. It's just something that's always in my heart. I really wanted that wrong to be righted because it was so close to me. Those kids were the first time I ever really engaged with white people. White people didn't come in black people's neighborhoods at that time. And for us to see white kids smiling in that neighborhood—instead of throwing things at us, bricks and rocks and banana peels and things, and calling us all kind of demeaning slang like "nigger" and "jigaboo"—that was dangerous at that time. It was a dangerous time for those kids to be in Meridian, Mississippi.

A lot of white kids who came down to work for civil rights, it was dangerous for them, too. Mind you, this was a period of time that there was real hatred in the air—white people didn't want black people to have rights, and they did everything they could to stop you from voting for these rights. Whatever it took, the whites did at that time in the South.

My dad was a landscaper and those civil rights workers created a lot of commotion around the city of Meridian at that time. It was a scary, scary atmosphere for anyone that was involved with them. And my dad and a lot other people from Meridian chose to take that challenge and hid those kids, from house to house, from church to church, in basements, in attics, in back rooms. And the same thing happened with us as well.

Being a little boy, you really didn't understand. You knew something was going on, but you had no idea about the toll that racism was taking in the South. Churches burned and you heard rumors of kids being beaten and that type of thing and how bad the police were. Our parents really tried to protect us as much as they could. All black parents did. You had curfews at a certain time of night and you had family curfews, too. You couldn't be out on the street and things because, I'm sorry, you could wind up hurt or even killed. You could definitely wind up missing if you were a black kid and you were found wandering the streets late at night, so it wasn't a good thing to do.

Mind you, the police departments and the mayors and the governors and everybody at this time in the Southern states were very, very bad people. You're talking about George Wallace. You're talking about Ross Barnett. You're talking about real bad people at this time—prominent people who are in control of situations and in control of government, so it was an awful time.

It was just a bad, bad situation. As I grew up I worked with my dad, who was a landscaper. This was his work all the way up until he died. This was our family business and I grew up with this job. At work, Daddy would often discuss with us what it was like growing up around this time, as black kids, as slave descendants. He taught us right from wrong. He taught us not to hate and to withdraw from any situation but, man, it was just hard. Even for me as a little-bitty boy it was real hard. Schools hadn't integrated or anything at that time. You had black school teachers in the black schools and the school was located near the house, so you were able to walk home. You live in an all-black community, so you weren't really in harm's way—but you were in harm's way. There were things going on in the South in those days—church burnings and that type of thing. I'm sorry, it was a very intimidating atmosphere.

At the same time, there was a lot of love and a lot of peace in the town that I grew up in, between the black communities. Blacks would kind of stick together a little bit more at this time. A lot of cohesiveness was going on between blacks. At that time in Mississippi, basically you were afraid of the law and the regulations and the rules that were surrounding your life.

Poverty brings this. Poorness brings this. But at the same time it brought a jelling, too. But as soon as these atmospheres started to evolve into integration and blacks and whites started going to school together, a little bit of change came. But it didn't come real fast.

I can remember what it was like growing up at that time, having a lot of siblings—five older brothers, two older sisters, and a younger sister who was killed in 1956, by my dad. My dad accidentally ran over his own daughter.

That same year, 1964, we moved to North Carolina. I really didn't know at the time why we moved. Daddy packed us all up and put us on this bus we used to own and we went to North Carolina. We took a few people with us and as we got up there we found work. Daddy was going to work in the tobacco fields. We stayed in North Carolina a little while, I don't remember how long.

When we got back to Mississippi those kids still hadn't been found.

They were looking for them all over the place. There were a lot of rumors, but who knows what was true and what wasn't. There were rumors about how these kids were found and that some Indians on the reservation had a lot to do with where the bodies were buried and how they came about finding them.

Mississippi Burning tells a lot of truth, but at the same time, living and growing up in that environment and growing up in the town and knowing the people that were involved with them—there was a lot more to the truth. There were a lot of things that weren't told about how and why those kids got killed, besides just going out protesting. That had a little bit to do with it, but there was more. It was a very angry atmosphere, and those kids were in harm's way every day that they were down here. A lot of churches were burned. A lot of people were getting beaten to tell where those kids hid or at houses where they stayed.

It happened a long time ago, but the presence was still there years later. James Chaney was a Meridian native. He was a black kid who was pushing for the rights of blacks in Meridian, and he was a close friend of my dad's younger brother, Frank Boyd. (Frank played ball, too. We all came out of black baseball, what you would call Negro League baseball—my dad, his younger brother, my mom's first cousins—was very prominent back then. As a matter of fact, it was the only peace that you had as a black community. On Saturdays and Sundays we'd watch and play baseball.)

To get back to the story of these kids being killed, it really affected my life, and still today it bothers me, because of the injustice behind something like that. And even though they eventually brought down the conspirators and everything, it still showed how bad things were that it took that long to bring about justice. It feels like right now, even though they don't keep people separate, you still have hatred in the South—just as abundant as it was many, many years ago.

• • •

Jumping ahead a bit, I have to tell you how I was almost connected to those killings in a different way.

After having a good year playing in the Florida State League in 1981, I went on over to Colombia, South America, and played winter ball until January '82. I got into some trouble down there when I was caught smoking pot on the beach by a policeman who looked like he was 15. It was, to say the least, an interesting time.

So I came back home to Meridian, and stayed for a couple of months before I got ready to head down to spring training. In the time that I was home I was trying to get my drivers license taken care of. I went to the DMV and they told me I had to get a valid social security card, because I didn't have the original one. So I'm there with the card they gave me, and I'm dealing with this black lady behind the counter. I thought that should have been sufficient. But she says no, and she's making me angry with her attitude, so I told her so. She's got a little authority, and she wants to throw it around.

I called her a "black bitch" right there in the office, and the next thing I knew I was under arrest. They were arresting me and I was arguing with them, and once they got me in the car they started saying stuff about how back in the day there was a place that they could take me.

It was a place called "the Mountains," and it was in Meridian, Mississippi. My dad said there were thousands of bodies—black bodies—buried in that place. Black kids would come up missing anywhere from the 1920s all the way up to the '70s, and possibly even the '80s. The kids that were supposedly taken to jail were beat to death, killed and buried in this place. It's pretty similar to what had happened to James Chaney and the two white workers back in '64.

So this is what the cop said to me: "I remember the day, and the time, that we used to be able to take a boy like you up on the Mountains, and you'd never be heard of again." And that's what they said to me. And let me tell you, I believed it, and I knew about it. And if I wasn't who I was—not so much the pro baseball player, mind you, but I got 3,500 relatives in the town that I live in, and my dad was a very, very prominent man, and my family was too—I might not be here today.

Plus, when I got into it with the cops, I made sure that I called my sister-in-law and told her where I was. So she came and picked me up downtown, and I told her what the cop had said to me. They would have killed me if it was just 15 years earlier, the cop said to me, while they were taking me up the elevator. And this is in Meridian, Mississippi. This is 1982, the same year I went to the major leagues for the Boston Red Sox!

And this is the type of thing that inspired my attitude to be the way it was against…I don't want to say all white people, but hey, it is what it is. One bad apple might spoil the whole bunch. That's the way I feel. Because when somebody says something to you like that, and you know that these kind of people have murdered kids, and buried them forever, that affects you.

Just because you can drink at the same water fountain, ride on the same buses, and all these types of things, those are not equal rights. Those are permanent rights. Those are things that are justified to every man. Be it whoever you are, or what walk of life you came from, rules and regulations and Jim Crow laws have disturbed life all the way up until today.

I'm still tormented by my past and it's hard to let go, because you can't let go of blackness.

Now, I come from three different bloods. The blood that runs through me is African, but it's also Irish and Native American; Choctaw, to be exact.

My great grandmother's name was Leona Pullos—that was her Indian name—and my great grandfather, Len Boyd, was born a slave. They met in Central Mississippi picking cotton, soy beans, corn, etc.

Back in that day a black man and an Indian could marry in the state of Mississippi, though neither race could marry a white. That was on my dad's side of the family, and that's how my family tree began.

The Irish blood began on my dad's mother's side of the family. You see, my great granddad, Bonner Coleman, he was white as snow. He had two families: a black family and a white family.

Back in those days, a lot of white men had two families, and that's where I come from. That's where my baseball comes from. Both sides of the family's genes were real strong in the game of baseball.

Coming from that type of background made me three different people. The hot blood would boil when I drank. That was the Indian in me showing up. The African blood that I carry made me strong in life, made it just about where I could endure anything that life could put out there. After all, I was a fourth-generation descendent of a slave. The white blood that flowed through me made it so I could perceive and understand the life of being part Indian and part African. I'm very proud of my heritage—all of my heritage. So no one can ever say that Dennis Boyd is a bigot! But still, I can't let go of how I really truly feel about life. These situations—and especially the situation of James Chaney, Andrew Goodman, and Michael Schwerner being killed with no mercy—they make you who you are. And times haven't changed as much as some people think. James Chaney is buried in Meridian, and every year someone takes a sledgehammer to his tombstone.

I'm still sad for the parents who will never see their kids again, and I'm still angry about the injustice they received from the Southern mentality of lawmakers, governors, lawyers, mayors, police departments, chiefs of police—most who weren't held accountable and still today aren't held accountable.

That's the early part of my years, when I really started to find out that I was a black kid and what it really meant.

When I walked into the bus station in '66 with my mom to pay some bills—that's where you paid your water bill, your electric bill, etc.—I'll never forget a white man behind the counter speaking to my mom like she was nothing. They didn't want you in the bus station—this is when they'd just passed the Civil Rights Act, but still written on the walls, just under one coat of paint, was prejudice and bigotry, just lurking around. Things hadn't changed just because the president had signed something. Civil rights didn't mean shit.

I was turning seven years old, just going into the second grade. I was a mama's boy, but I also had older brothers and sisters, which kind of made it sweet because there was a lot of love in the house. A *lot* of love—but I also have to say it was very dysfunctional at home because of the slave mentality. Regardless of what had happened, my dad was raised by a dad who was the grandson of a sharecropper, so you couldn't expect much intelligence or direction in a Southern home at that time because blacks were too busy trying to make it, day in and day out.

We couldn't love and care for siblings, like you see today. It was very different. As kids, we learned a lot on our own—a lot of good things, but a lot of bad things as well. One thing that was always around, though, was that you were a black kid and you were a slave descendant. Your life was in despair and your home was in chaos and your neighborhood was a mess. Illiteracy, poverty, they were everywhere.

When schools integrated, it seemed like blacks segregated themselves from each other. Some blacks wanted integration and some blacks didn't, so it created a split in attitude, where some blacks were, "Whatever this white man gives us is good enough," and some blacks were, "We don't want that. We want true rights. We want true respect."

Some blacks would go for anything, and very many blacks did, because it was about survival. You came up in a poor-ass atmosphere, and it humbled everyone differently. I'm still black today, and regardless of where I went in life, nothing is going to take away the fucking despair and the things that I felt growing up. That's what transformed me into the person I am today.

I had to get over a lot of hurt, a lot of misfortunes, a lot of things that had to do with just growing up as a kid in Mississippi. It's hard for you to believe in the God that was given to you. It's hard for you believe, being a slave, in the religion that was given to you. It's hard to believe in the name that's been given to you. It's hard to be the person who you really are when you are made to be someone else.

You can't identify with your culture. You can't identify with being an African anymore. We're Europeanized, so all the things that we've learned we learned from a slave master and those things led to the type of people we are today. Nothing can take that away. It's just hard to be able to function in a world where you don't feel like you belong and you don't have a home. The home that you have is the home that was given to you. The name that you have is the name that was given to you. Not one good thing came out of slavery.

Today I still don't feel that integration is a good thing. Integration gave white people an upper hand; it didn't give us a hand at all. The white man is in control, and as black people growing up we learned that that's just the way it is. This is what it's about. That's a tough thing to swallow. To live with, "For you to prosper, this is the way you have to prosper." For you to go on in life you have to suck up, you have to forgive and forget, and that's heartbreaking. For you to give up everything that you are so that you can try to become something that somebody else wants you to be in order for you to get along, in order for you to receive the civil benefits from the country that made you a slave descendant in the first place, that's a bad thing.

The first day of school in the first grade, I jumped out of the classroom window and literally ran back home. I was so used to being under my mom's care, and when she took me to school and told me I was going to stay there it scared me to death. So I ran back home until I figured out you have to go to school.

I changed elementary schools, and in the third grade I had a beautiful teacher who really loved me. Miss Williams was special. At the time I was a really sensitive kid. I cried a lot. I was a spoiled-ass kid. I came from a lot of sisters and brothers. I wanted my way and when I didn't have my way I would have fits.

I was just like that. They called it "spoiled" but no one can really spoil black kids, not when you get your ass beaten that much. It was a real good year, 1967. We didn't have T-ball; we had little league baseball. If you were good enough to play and make the team, it didn't matter how old you were. We didn't have these coach-pitch leagues and these types of things. You just had to get out there with the big guys and that's pretty much what made me the ballplayer I became, having to get out there in competition with kids who were four, five, and six years older. Playing baseball, basketball, wrestling, tackle football, and everything. We were rough kids growing up in the South. You had to be very physical, because pretty much everything was settled that way.

There was a lot of fighting going on. That's just the Southern mentality. Boys are tough in the South. To get your way you pretty much had to hold your ground. You had to be able to put up some dukes, even as a little boy. Kids were like that, black kids especially. Schools weren't integrated. Black kids, we were very aggressive kids. It wasn't anything for you to come home with your nose bloody or shirt torn or anything like that. That's just the way the environment was. We were Southern kids. We were outdoor kids and we settled things with our little fists. But it was all right; the next day we were playing on the playgrounds and the best of friends.

I still have friends today that I fought with every day growing up. It's just the way it was. It was preparing you, getting you ready for life. Today, parents would be panicking and shit, but when we were kids it was preparing us for life and I wouldn't take any of those things back, because of how tough it made me.

This was also around the time I started going to work with my dad in the summers to really experience what work was. Like I said, he was a landscaper, and he'd haul sod, he'd haul concrete, he'd haul wood and logs, anything and everything just to make a living. And we were expected to do the same, to go out there as a family. My older brothers, Skeeter, Steve, Mike, Don, and Neal, right on down to myself; along with my first cousins, Larry and Charles; and my dad's sister's kids, we all pretty much grew up in the family business. This is how we took care of home and this is how we shared money and food and Christmases, and a bunch more. There was a lot of love in the neighborhood, outside of knowing that if you wandered off too far you could get your tail beat by some wild white kids who were out looking for some black people to stomp.

That type of thing was going on, too, so you kind of had to watch yourself. But as long as you stayed where you were supposed to be you were all right, even though every now and then you would venture out and you would get into things you shouldn't get into.

We used to deliver pies for this lady who baked all kinds of little cream pies and pecan pies and sold them. My brothers and I would deliver these pies to different houses, different neighborhoods. And sometimes you would have to walk through white neighborhoods and white kids would sic their dogs on us and call us names and throw bricks and rocks at us, and every now and then you would have to fight with them. They were considered poor white trash and poor white trash hated you worse than anybody because they felt like, "Hey, if I ain't better than anybody else I'm better than a nigger," so we heard that cliché growing up all the time.

I was really getting into art around that time, too. I had a couple of brothers and sisters who were pretty good with pens and paint, my brother Don and my sister Gayle especially, were very good. I kind of took that up from them and they showed me a few things. As I grew older, it became a passion and I've stayed with it up until today. Every now and then I catch myself doing something with a little paint here and there. I can see myself getting back into it, but right now baseball is still the king in my life.

2: Baseball, Family, and Integration

"Jackie Robinson was a

modern-day Shaka Zulu."

Baseball, Family, and Integration

In 1969, I became very, very conscious of the game of baseball. I played little league baseball, and I really started to fall in love with the game, basically through my brothers, through my family. This is the time that I'm really starting to go to the little league field and I'm really starting to learn to play the game with my friends. We would go to different houses and get kids to play pickup games anywhere we could find an empty lot—whether it was grass, concrete, or whatever, we were going to play some baseball on it.

We broke a lot of windows in the neighborhood growing up—car windows, house windows, church windows. Whether we were hitting or throwing, those windows had to go, because we were playing baseball and we were in love with it. We participated in a lot of other things at the time. School was a priority, basically because schools hadn't integrated yet and the black teachers knew that for us to prosper or to be anything in life, we needed to learn. Living under the despair of being a slave descendant, you had to get this man's education and you had to know how his world worked, so black teachers did care for us. They *did* teach us and they *did* tell us about who we were and what we were going to be.

That soon stopped because by the time 1970 and '71 came around the schools integrated. Like I said, some thought it was good when schools integrated, but me, even as a young boy, I didn't like it. Why? First of all, you're putting us somewhere where people don't want us to be. People talking about civil rights this and civil rights that. I've always been a person to say, "No man has to give me no right, I'm born with that right." To drink at a water fountain, or to ride at the front or back of a bus was irrelevant. It didn't prove to us that we were second or that we had equality—those are not the things that give you equality.

Who you are gives you equality; not what a man tells you. You're not equal to him when he can tell you where you can't drink at and then all of a sudden drop a law that tells you that you can. Where is the equality in that? You can't tell *yourself* where to drink water? You can't tell *yourself* where to go on a bus? Because they own the bus, they own the water, they own *everything*.

These people didn't want us in their country anymore after they abolished slavery. They didn't want to have anything to do with us. And now what do they do? Give us the poorest education, give us the poorest part of the world, the poorest part of the country, the scraps off of the table. Nothing's changing for a kid who said, "I have to get out of here. I have to do something to become somebody." You're only becoming somebody for *him* and not for you.

I don't feel like I accomplished nothing by becoming a major league ballplayer, because I didn't play in the Negro Leagues. I didn't get a chance to play among my peers and be respected by my peers. I didn't want to be like other blacks and accept it. I really didn't want to think and feel like Jackie Robinson one bit.

I couldn't have been Jackie Robinson. Not for a day!

See, up the street from me was a Negro League baseball player. His name was Roy Dawson. When I got older I was going to build a ballfield, and I was going to name it Dawson, McNair, and Webb Stadium. Skeeter Webb and Eric McNair played back in the '30s. They're from Meridian and I was going to name my ballfield after one Negro Leaguer and two prominent guys who played back in the era of Babe Ruth. That's what was on my blueprint.

Mr. Roy Dawson was a left-handed pitcher back in the day. Way I heard it, he beat Satchel Paige every goddamn time he faced him. Word was that Roy Dawson was badder than Satchel Paige! Well, Mr. Roy grew up three houses from me, and my dad used to tell us when we were little that Mr. Roy played professional baseball. We didn't know about Negro League baseball as little boys, not until Daddy explained it to us at eight or nine years old. He used to say, "That man was a pro."

We didn't know what he was talking about, because we figured pros were white. We thought pros were named Ted Williams, Ty Cobb, and Al Kaline. We thought those were the only pros. We didn't know of blacks being pros back in the day. As kids growing up in the '60s we knew about Jackie, and that was pretty much it. But some of the older kids and my older brothers, they knew the real background because some of the men that my older brothers grew up batboying and playing for were still playing. One of them just died in 2011: Early Moore, a Negro Leaguer, at 80 years old. I actually played *with* him. He's my mom's first cousin, and not only did he play for the Indianapolis ABCs and the Indianapolis Clowns, he was also a Globetrotter. He was a Negro Leaguer and he was one of the last living ones.

Now Mr. Roy Dawson was a Negro Leaguer, and he played before Jackie. He played against Babe Ruth, he faced Dizzy Dean; he knew all them cats. Dizzy Dean grew up down the road from me, in Wiggins, Mississippi, 30 miles away from where I was born and raised. Negro Leaguers played all-white teams down there all the time in the winter. Mr. Roy Dawson told me about Jackie Robinson when I was a 12-year-old kid. So one day, when Daddy and I were working side-by-side in the sod pasture, I asked him about Jackie. He told me, "He really didn't do anything good for our race."

I'm like, "Daddy, he played in the major leagues."

"No, Baby, we had our own league and we had our own individuality and Jackie didn't know that he was making a business deal to sell his people—like slavery all over again. Jackie Robinson was a modern-day Shaka Zulu—he was the King who sold his own people into slavery—so all Jackie did was sell us to Major League Baseball the same way."

That's the way my daddy described it. He said all Jackie did was take the power away from us and give it to them. So now we're in their league, where they can control the commerce, they can control the welfare, they can control everything, and now we've become a commodity.

Branch Rickey had an ultimate plan. He knew that he needed a man who could take what was about to happen, but there was something else going on here. Negro League baseball was thriving and this was almost like the Civil War mentality all over again. Negroes were thriving and making money—even though most of the owners were white, Negro League ball was a major factor for black businesses who backed these teams—and Branch Rickey broke all that up.

I am proud of Jackie but not proud *for* Jackie. There's a difference.

And when we look back, it looks like Branch Rickey gave blacks a chance to play baseball, but we were already playing baseball. So let's tell the damn truth. Don't make it seem like he gave us a chance to play baseball. We were playing with whites way back in the 1880s and 1890s. It wasn't like they made it out to be. Back in the 1920s, Kenesaw Mountain Landis was the commissioner of baseball, and in my opinion he'd been someone who helped to keep the Jim Crow laws in place. We'd been playing baseball for a long time and Branch Rickey broke all that up. He didn't just take Jackie.

All of this stuff, it made for a difficult situation to be put into as a kid growing up, not knowing really who you are, what you are, having to become something that you didn't want to become. I was forced to be something that I'm not. All the people in the world that don't have a home, we're supposed to get over that. That's the worst thing in the world that a person can say to me. Get over being owned and them controlling your life and prospering from everything that slavery brought forth and enhanced. You're going to tell me to get over that? "You should be over that," is the biggest lie that was ever fucking told.

This was also the time, in 1969, that I wrote a school paper for one of my favorite teachers, Miss Cole, my fifth-grade teacher. You know how teachers are always asking "What do you want to be when you grow up?" Well, shit, when I was nine years old I wrote that I wanted to be a baseball player. And I'll be damned, almost 20 years later she had kept this paper and she gave it back to me, and she said it was the most unusual and special thing— that a kid would say he wanted to be something so improbable and then go out and do it.

She said, "I could tell when you were a little boy that you were going to be what you wanted to be." It was just in me at that time. It was a good time.

Then, all of a sudden, they forced integration on us. Integration basically made us "niggers," even though it was a time that everyone was supposed to be trying to jell and everything. You wouldn't put two people who are having this type of difficulty with each other together and just tell them to get along and expect it to instantly happen.

I was hurt by it because I was really sensitive to someone looking down on me because of the color of my skin. I still haven't gotten over that today. What would make a person think that the color of their skin made them more worthy of belonging in the world?

These are the type of things you feel as a black kid growing up. I can't say all blacks felt this way, though, because you did have the blacks who said, "Hey, we have to give in. If we can't beat them, we have to join them." That's the attitude that brought what we have today. Today you have the type of black man who would do anything for money, the type that would turn in his own brother for money, *has* turned in his own brother for money.

It's been happening since slavery. It would be a slave that would report other slaves trying to run away. That slave mentality is still around and exists today. I've experienced it myself, because I've been told by blacks, "Hey, Dennis, if you don't keep your mouth quiet then you're going to get kicked out the game," and, "Man, you making it bad for us." These are the blacks who have given in to the system. I was wasn't one of them, so I stood out. But that's still bringing down your race, because that's telling the white man, "Hey, if *that* black man won't do it, we'll find a black that will."

There are blacks out there who are ready to take on a religion that wasn't theirs or take on a European name that wasn't theirs, and really not fight about it, just go along with it. Those blacks who say, "I don't care where I come from, I don't care what happened back then," they should be ashamed of themselves. They're ashamed of being slave descendants, ashamed of being black. They're ashamed of it, so they want to take that shame away by saying, "I'll do it, I'll be it, I'll belong and maybe you will accept me."

Integration was a bad thing. Integration made them prosper and made us not prosper. It gave them back the same control that they had over us in bondage and slavery. So the old ways of, "All the laws that I make you're going to abide by or I'll incarcerate you," grew into "I'm going to put drugs on the streets and you're going to buy them and you're going to sell them and then I'm going to put you in jail for it." That's what integration brought. If you put someone with somebody that don't like them, how's it going to turn out? Well, we saw how it turned out.

That's basically what it is, and I'm expected to abide by it. And if I don't then I'm a rebellious person and I don't respect authority. But all you're really saying is that I don't respect the master. I don't respect that attitude of "You do what I say or I will chain and shackle your ass just like I did 250 years ago. If you mess around here I got something *for* you. I got a system that revolves around incarcerating you and putting you in jail and taking your life away."

Nothing's changed for the black man. The only thing they changed is how we perceive things. They've deceived us, just like they've been doing since we've been here. We've gone for trickery and we've been deceived and most black people don't even know it. They'll say to me, "You're the one being deceived. I'm doing what I'm supposed to do. I'm going to get educated. I'm going to go to college and I'm going to come out and I'm going to be a professor."

The problem is, you're still saying you want to work in their world, you ain't saying you want to be in your own world. See, to me something's wrong in that. I don't want your name. I don't want your religion. I want to know who *I* am as an individual. As a black man, I never got a chance to be an individual because every

31

time that I spoke out about choices that had to do with white people, somebody blew it down. There's black people saying, "Don't speak up like that." There's white people saying, "Nigger, you *can't* say that," and "You're *not* going to do that," and "If you rebel against us this is what will happen to you."

This is what my dad and them went through. This is what all blacks, on back since we've been over here in this country, went through. I wanted to be one of the kids who grew up and tried to make a change in all of this. But the more I tried to make a change the harder it became.

I mean, I tried to do it even in elementary school. I wanted to be a kid that, as soon as the schools integrated, I was the first one to let them know, "Hey, I'm not going for this." Even at 11 years old I knew the difference. I knew what respect was, and I knew that I came from a hard-working family and deserved respect. My people weren't in welfare lines. We didn't ask for anything and we didn't want them to give us anything.

That type of attitude made blacks around us become envious. As a matter of fact, some of them hated us for not wanting to be poor, hated us for not wanting to be ignorant niggers. Blacks hated us because they wanted us to be the same thing that they were: uneducated and docile. If you got out of that, it was, "Nigger, who do you think you are? You think you better than we are?" That's the attitude that's been created through slavery. Blacks are always trying to pull other blacks down, because it makes other blacks look bad. Where I came from, instead of other blacks pulling for you, saying, "Go out and succeed in life and be something," they were saying, "Don't be shit."

Even my daddy came up with that mentality. He had it with my brothers. My dad wanted to take my siblings out of school, because he thought school was a waste of time.

"What a black man need an education for?" my dad said. That's the way my dad thought about life. If it wasn't for my mom stepping in and saying, "These babies have to have it," who knows how things would have turned out. My daddy wasn't educated and he really thought that education had nothing to do with putting a dollar in your pocket. He really thought that if you kissed enough ass and you worked hard enough, a white man would feed you. He was defiant about that and it really made us angry with him. Even though he worked hard, and we worked right beside him, we didn't want to be raised with that mentality.

Even that, the chaos at home, that's the slave mentality. You have some blacks, some siblings, they fight against each other. If one succeeds, goes out and becomes something in life, and the other one doesn't, there's envy. At least in my family there was. My dad brought us up like that. He pitted us against each other, in everything that we did. If one brother was better than another at something, he instructed you to get just as good at it.

That kind of competition is only healthy if it's positive. But it wasn't. It was negative, and it created a feeling between me and my brothers that we didn't want to see each other succeed in life. Even up to today, we don't want to see each other succeed, because of that slave mentality.

It was like the rat mentality and that's how blacks were being raised—being raised poor and being raised in poor water areas, flood zones, everything that could come with poverty. Fuck, Ethiopia was like Meridian, Mississippi, and all those other little towns down through there, where you got rebel towns hanging every-goddamn-where and rebel flags were "distinguishing the type of people that we are and the type of people that you are,"— and as long as we keep that flag flying over our cities down south there will always be segregation in people's minds. "We don't give a shit if we go to work with you, or eat with you or even every now and then let a black come into the church with us. We don't want to be a part of you. And it still goes on today.

• • •

It was in '71 or '72 that the schools integrated, and it was my brothers who were the first blacks on the integrated high school baseball team to actually play. They weren't the first ones to integrate the team; they were the first ones to actually be on the ballfield. There were a couple other blacks out there. Lemmie Kelly and Leander Scott were two very good black ballplayers. Lemmie, especially, could have played in the major leagues for anybody. But at the time that these kids were growing up, there were no black baseball players in the city at the high school level.

When integration came in, blacks were awarded the right to play basketball. Of course they're going to be awarded the right to play basketball. And then blacks are going to be awarded the right to play football. Baseball was considered a white man's game and still is today, so the mentality around it was that blacks weren't intelligent enough to play baseball, especially at certain positions. So my brothers were the first ones to come in there and move that stigma out, that negative, demeaning attitude that so many people weren't really conscious of at that time. I take it back, they were conscious.

We knew the stereotypes: blacks can't pitch, blacks only play the outfield. Because, you know, blacks can run and jump and that type thing, but when it came to the thinking man's positions, like behind the plate, even Roy Campanella couldn't show them that. It was just clichés that were still thrown around, especially in the South. They knew we were better ballplayers and better athletes; they just didn't want to give us a chance because they knew we'd knock so many white kids out of the game.

Back in '68, when schools hadn't integrated, my brother Mike was asked to come and play football at an all-white junior high school when he was in the eighth or ninth grade. He was the only black at the school. They wanted him purely for football, because he was a big, strong, fast kid, a super athlete. But in the process, going to an all-white school, my brother was fighting every day. Every single day he'd come home bloody because he fought kids. My mom wanted the best for him, but at the same time she was worried to death that one night he wouldn't make it home.

He was on an all-white football team and his *own team* was against him, even when he was running the football. They wouldn't block for him, that type thing, trying to get him hurt on the field. But the coaches wanted him to play because he could help this program be a winning program, because he was the best athlete in the whole city. So much so that a few years later he'd helped integrate the high school baseball team when integration came in *legally*. Because, you see, it was still illegal in '68. This school integrated when they wanted it, when it helped them. "We want this black in this school because we have a use for him, but the other blacks can't come because we don't have no use for them."

A few years later, Mike, along with my brother Steve and my brother Don, went out and made the high school baseball team. Within two years they had won the state championship. I don't know the record, but I do know that Meridian High won a state championship in the early '70s with my brothers playing the biggest roles.

My brother Steve was a senior at the time, so he only got a chance to play one year. From what I understand, the coach put him and Don at the same position. I was in the sixth grade when this happened and I used to go to their practices and watch my brothers. At the time, there were some good white kids out there, but there were some bad white kids, too. Bill Marchant, the coach, had to take on a heavy load, because he had to integrate a team and no white person in the whole city wanted any blacks on Meridian High. He had to go through that, and he caught much hell putting my brothers on the team.

He got all types of threats for putting my brothers on the team, and when they won a state championship, believe it or not it wasn't even enough. But here we come, a few years later, my brother Neil and I. My brothers had set the stage for the blacks to come out and really be looked at as baseball players.

My brothers, when they were there, would talk to other blacks who were just as good as they were and ask them why they didn't come out for the team and they would just say, "Man, we can't come out there and put up with that white man. We can't come out there and put up with them racist white boys." That was a bad atmosphere because a lot of good ballplayers missed the opportunity to play, because high school was the way for you to be seen playing baseball. Mind you, the Negro Leagues were over with and so was signing baseball players out of sandlot leagues.

You have to be in high school and play or you're not going to be seen by the scouts. My brothers knew that. That paved the way for my brother Neil and I to go off and play university ball. Mike was drafted. Steve was considered for the draft, but he only played one year of high school ball so he went off into the navy, but he was a damn good ballplayer. I can't compare them all, but I like to say that I take a back seat to every last one of them.

My oldest brother, Skeeter, finished school in '69. I don't know if he graduated high school. I want to say that my daddy took him out of school, and that kind of pissed off my mama and my brother. He talks about it to this day, about the mentality that my dad had, that blacks didn't need school, they needed to be at work. We have to put food on the table and that was the only thing that was important.

My dad knew that his boys had great baseball talent, but no man believed that his kid was going to the pros. Even though Jackie Robinson had gone to the major leagues, my dad wasn't under the illusion that other black kids would be going unless they were like Jackie, which we weren't.

When you talk about the few ballplayers that came out of there, they were few and far in between and you really didn't know about them or even hear about them. We knew about Satchel Paige, we knew about Willie Mays, Tommie Agee, Hank Aaron, and Amos Otis. We knew about the elite ballplayers, but there were thousands of ballplayers who didn't get a chance to play because they weren't given the opportunities.

• • •

My brother Mike was the inspiration that got me to the major leagues. His story also helped me get kicked out of the major leagues. I was always so bitter about Mike's career, knowing that Mike probably would have been one of the best fucking baseball players who ever lived. That might just be my point of view, it might not, but if you saw my brother as a kid you would have damn near seen Superman on a baseball field.

He was like Bo Jackson and Dave Winfield. He was a mixture of about five or six guys all in one and he was as strong and quick as all of them, and he had probably the greatest arm that I've ever seen—and I played major league baseball. I've seen some great arms in the pros, and before and after my tenure, and I still haven't seen an arm like my brother Mike's!

Mike was something like 19–2 in his senior season and his team won the state championship. He had some crazy, mind-

37

blowing stats. He was considered one of the best pitchers in the country at that time. He possessed a 95 mph fastball and he could run, hit, and pitch. He was much bigger in stature than me.

So what happened to Mike? He was the best ballplayer in the family, and probably in the state of Mississippi at the time. He was drafted by the Dodgers in '73, but he ended up not receiving a contract. And why? Because he got a white girl pregnant. Mike was my inspiration, but Mike lost his career, and he lost it because the schools were integrated. White girls wanted some black boys and they didn't give a damn what happened. A lot of them got kicked out of their own homes.

Mike got the girl he was seeing pregnant in '71 and my nephew was born in '72. His name is Michael, and he had to be raised in our house, with us, because the girl's parents didn't want the baby. That's the bottom line.

I'll never forget when we all went out to the hospital to see the baby being born. We, as the black family, knew that she was pregnant by my brother Mike, but her family didn't, so it caused a big commotion at the hospital. I'll never forget her dad saying, "That's a nigger's baby, that's not my goddamn grandchild." I'll never forget him and my dad arguing and about to get into a fist fight and having to bring the police out there and everything. It was just a bad, bad thing.

It split the town, because the town eventually found out. Mind you, you're talking about a city that's probably, at the time, 50/50 or 60/40 blacks to whites. No integration. Total segregation. It got rough for Mike and us, as well as for the girl and her family. Her parents eventually ended up leaving the city.

It also broke up Mike's career. All the major league scouts shunned him when they found out that he'd had a baby by a white girl. He went through all kinds of things to get on the ballfield. He was drafted by the Dodgers, but was never put in the scouting bureau, and if you're not put in the bureau, nobody's going to bring you a contract. So Mike ended up going to a small junior college instead of going to play ball that summer, and in the fall he started at Chipola Junior College down in Florida.

His first son, Michael, was born when I was 12 years old. Mike was getting ready to play ball at Chipola, which was a place that he shouldn't have been. He went down there in the early '70s, and there'd been rumors of a lynching there only a couple years earlier. That lets you know the world Mike was led into.

Mike was basically told to go play at Chipola, because it would be a good opportunity for him to continue his career. He was only 18 years old and had never really been away from home and you're sending him to probably the most racist state in the union at the time, Florida, to go play college baseball.

While he was down there, Mike told me things that continue to hurt me to today. His teammates treated him like garbage down there. They basically just tormented him. To this day, Mike is still not together, and I hurt every time I think about what this time in his life did to him.

Racism broke up my family, tortured my brother's life, tortured all our lives. It really took a lot away from my brothers and my family.

What's to blame? Slavery's to blame—and even more than that, slave owners. That mentality is never going to change. If you didn't want something to be brought back to you, you should never have done it in the first place, because you're going to be reminded by Dennis Boyd—every day, all my life, how it was to be a black kid, growing up in Mississippi, and growing up in this great country called the United States of America.

That's why I never really trusted anyone in Major League Baseball. I never really enjoyed my time in Major League Baseball because of these feelings, the manipulation of blacks and how we were supposed to act if we wanted to belong. "Nigger, be thankful you are getting paid and you do what we say and don't speak out of line." It's just ignorance and bigotry.

Mike was told that he'd never play in the big leagues because he did a forbidden thing, and a nigger can't do that. It cursed my whole family, and it curses them until today. It's something that my family will never live down. It took away Mike's career, and then it basically took the careers away from my other brothers, Don and Neal, as well.

• • •

The Cardinals drafted my brother Don in '73.

Don came back with some stories of pro ball. He signed a contract out of high school and went to play in the Cardinals organization in Sarasota, Florida, in the Gulf Coast League. Don swung the bat pretty well. From what the stats show, Don played some good baseball in rookie ball that season, but he was released that same year.

With the kind of talent that he had, they don't release you the year they draft you. But Don had the mentality that he wasn't taking no shit. Plus, he was coming to the pros right after Mike, something he said he was reminded of every day, by every scout, every coach, everyone who knew the two were brothers.

Don said that one of his coaches in the Gulf Coast League was an old-time racist, and he told me something that coach said to him that still hurts him today.

One of his white teammates took him out to the bars one night. Now, Don wasn't a drinker or troublemaker; he wasn't any of those things. Don was a very intelligent man, and he didn't take shit from nobody, but really he was just a strong-ass country boy who could play good baseball. Don told me that the next day the coach put his finger in his face and told him, "You're not going to get to the major leagues, just like that black-ass brother of yours. I'm telling you this because I heard that you was out with some white girls last night. You're just like your brother."

The Cardinals picked my brother Mike up after a year or so of being out of baseball. They signed him and put him with Don for a little bit, but before you knew it both of them were out of the game and back home.

This was in the same year that my mom got very sick and we didn't know what was wrong with her. She was in and out of the hospital for a few years and me, as a little boy in the eighth grade, I had to live in the hospital *with* my mom. At the time I didn't know that her sickness was actually due to her drinking throughout the years. The doctors in Mississippi had given up on her. They couldn't figure out what was going on, and they told her that she only had a few days to live This was just after Don got released from pro ball (he never tried to get back in or anything) and went to work with my dad.

My mom's brother, Jesse McCoy, lived up in St. Louis. He told Don that we should try to get my mom to a hospital up there. He said those doctors up there could find out what was wrong with her and save her life.

Meridian is about an eight-hour drive from St. Louis. Don did it in five.

As a matter of fact, from what he told me he drove so fast that he got pulled over by a highway patrolman with my mom laid out in the back seat of the car. My mom only had so many hours to live and if he didn't get her to the hospital she would be dead by the next day. The highway patrolman escorted my brother all the way to St. Louis, driving at speeds over 100 mph all the way to the emergency room.

It saved my mom's life for at least another 15 years. This was '73 and she died in '89. It gave her a second chance in life, though she didn't quit drinking.

Don got married around this time, but he would still come by the house and check on my brother Neal and me, because my other siblings were grown and gone and had their own families. He would check in on us, making sure that we had clothes and food on the table. In the summer, I would work with Don and Dad, and so would my brother Neal and my cousin Larry and other people in the family. That's the way we made a living. In the summer we worked, and then went to school in the winter, and even during the Christmas holidays it was back to work, going out and making money for Christmas gifts and things.

It was a good life, but it was a *hard* life. It was worth it, because it made me tough as nails. As hard as it was, I wouldn't give up what my dad showed me about how to survive and how to take care of myself.

"Baseball," Dad said to me, "would be the easiest thing that you ever did in your life. It would be like sweepin' the floor."

And he wasn't lying. Nothing in life could compare to how I grew up as a kid. There ain't a burden out there that they can lay on me that's tougher than what my dad showed. Anything that I got into in life, I just looked back on what my dad taught me and I came up out of that shit boxing like a champ.

3: Oil Can

"He's *our* nigger!"

Oil Can

1975 was the first year I played high school baseball. I played under Bill Marchant, the high school coach at the time. A little bit of the racism and things had gone away—but believe me, just a little bit. When my brother Mike and them were playing in the early '70s they were being called "Nigger, Nigger, Nigger," on every high school field they played. Some of the same things happened to me, too, but it wasn't as bad as it had been.

This was when I started to learn what the game of baseball was. I really learned the game of baseball from Coach Marchant, especially the mental part of the game, which we didn't know as black kids. We knew the physical part. We could run and catch and throw—all the basics of the game—but we didn't know the strategy of the game. That's what he taught me: how to really see the game, how to think on the field, and how to create favorable situations. I'm thankful to God that Coach Marchant was there at the beginning of my life in baseball.

See, that's the thing about black ballplayers at that time. We would physically match anybody, but as soon as we got on the ballfield against white teams, they'd play with strategy. Even white teams I played growing up, they were more sound mentally. They knew the game, knew the fundamentals. We'd out-do them in physical things—we were stronger, we were faster, but for some reason we couldn't hit this pitcher, couldn't correct for this bunt or that shift, so we didn't get a chance to show our shit, because they were smarter ballplayers.

I learned the game of baseball from a white man. I didn't learn it from a black man. Coach Marchant taught us about bunt plays, taught us about the cutoff man, how to run a rundown, the mental part of the game. The kids in the neighborhood didn't know one goddamn thing about nothing like that.

So we started hearing the lingo. You have to understand, my dad and them were illiterate, so they passed the game down to us physically. They couldn't pass down the knowledge of *how* to play the game. It wasn't until Coach Marchant that I learned the other side of baseball.

Even with all that, we had mixed feelings about Bill Marchant. I mean, he's a white man, he's a white coach, coaching in Mississippi. But he had to live two lives. I think he learned to love my family. I know he respected my family and knew what kind of background we came from. He knew that my mom had been sick and he was there for me and Neal. He bought our spikes and things like that.

That was about the time when my daddy left us, and that's when mentors, like a high school coach, stepped in. We were a bit ashamed, to tell you the truth, to have someone buy something for us, knowing that we had a daddy who was working hard and who made money.

But Daddy was gone, so Bill Marchant stepped in and I love him for that today. But like I say, I still have mixed feelings toward Coach Marchant because of the earlier years with my brothers Don, Mike, and Steve. As I grew up, though, I learned that he was put in a very difficult situation. Hell, he could've been killed. That's seriously how it was—not harmed, not threatened, but literally *killed* for putting my brothers on the team. That's how strong the hatred was, and it definitely applied to a white man who showed any kind of encouragement or love for a black kid. Bill Marchant was tough as nails—yes he was—for standing there for my family, and I'll always appreciate that.

Years back, when my brothers integrated the high school baseball team, there was one incident between Coach Marchant and my family.

I was in the sixth grade and my brothers were playing high school ball. They'd gone to play one of the county schools, Northeast Lauderdale.

This one particular night, my mom and dad came to the game, but Coach Marchant didn't know they were there. The other team was ranked lower than us, they weren't a Meridian High–class level of baseball. That night they were, though. That night they whooped up Meridian High pretty good. Coach Marchant put in a second-string team but they couldn't hold these guys.

So then he wanted to put in my brother Mike to hold them down, but Mike had just pitched. Mike said no and Steve backed him up, and Coach Marchant ended up kicking my brothers off the team that night. He suspended them indefinitely and even made them walk home, said they couldn't even ride on the bus back with the team. Of course, he didn't know that my parents were there at the game. A big commotion came about when they got suspended.

I'll never forget a couple days later, when my mom came and picked me up from elementary school. It was about a mile or so from the high school, and the high school team was practicing. So she brought me down to the high school gym and told me to run across to the practice field and tell Coach Marchant to come to the car, she wants to talk to him.

When he came to the car my mom spoke to him. Now, Mom kept a pistol with her everywhere she went. I don't want to say that she threatened him to put my brothers back on the team, but I tell you, they were back on the team the next day. And they won the state championship that year.

If you ask me, I'd say yes, she would have shot him. After speaking to my brothers like he did, as well as some of the things he said to the newspapers about them, yes I think she would have. The way the newspapers reported it—like they were the worst thing that ever happened to that school—that just pissed my mom off real bad. My dad was at work when my mom went to handle it. He basically told my mom to handle anything like that, and believe me, she took care of business.

In '76, I was in the 11th grade. That's when I really prospered on the baseball field and found out how much I love this game. Even though I had a lot of learning to do, I was realizing how good I could be. I'd developed a very good curveball, and every day I was getting harder and harder to hit.

That was the year that we went to the state playoffs. It was a damn good baseball team, but the experiences of '76 weren't all that different from when my brothers played, because we still had to play in towns like Gulfport and Natches, Mississippi, where I was called "Nigger" every day and every night.

I remember this one time when we were on the Mississippi coast, in Pascagoula, getting ready to play in the state playoffs. I was pitching that night, and I was the only black player on the whole field. The umpire was a big black man—I mean like Shaquille O'Neal big. This brother was about 6'10", like 280 pounds! Then there was this little frail umpire out at second. A Barney Fife–looking motherfucker. He's a little guy—I'll never forget—and with that mean Southern look, too.

Before the game, Coach had a meeting and told us that it was going to be a hostile atmosphere that night because I was pitching. "Dennis," he said, "don't worry about nothing, everything's going to be all right." Even Coach Marchant didn't know how bad it was going to be, and he was from that town. After the meeting was over, Edgar Corley, the right fielder made me wait in the clubhouse. Everybody else was going to the field, and I was kind of nervous but I was already preparing myself. I knew that when I got mad it would take away the nervousness. Edgar came to me and said, "Don't worry shit about shit tonight. You can pitch this here. We wouldn't even be here tonight if it wasn't for you. You go out and do what you have to do. Don't worry about nothing."

Edgar and I walked to the field, and as we went through the crowd I could feel little rock pebbles hitting me. Edgar's saying, "That's all right. It's okay." He was walking around me, and then some of my teammates came and they were walking with me, making sure that nobody got up on me. They walked me right down to the field.

First inning of the game, the kids in the other dugout started up with that racist shit. I was pitching good and setting them down, and there were getting more and more worked up. Then, in the third or fourth inning, I gave up a double. Now this kid, once he's standing behind me on second base, he starts calling me a nigger.

My shortstop called time out, and he walked over to the kid and said, "Hey, you stop calling him that. The only person that can call him a nigger is us—he's *our* nigger!" Then he turned to the umpire and said, "You better stop him from calling him that." The Barney Fife umpire just stood there with his arms folded. He didn't say a word, didn't even look back.

While I'm going into my stretch, that kid on second is still talking to me. "Hey, Nigger, Nigger, Nigger, we going to get you tonight. You little black bastard." And then their dugout and fans got in on it, chanting "Nigger" at me, and my shortstop's getting ready to fight that kid on second. But I just kept pitching, kept mowing them down, and they just got louder and louder. I was crying while I was pitching, but those boys just kept striking out and going back to the dugout, and when they got there they joined the others in screaming at me. They were standing up at the fence, yelling all kinds of shit, and every time I'd hear it I'd strike out another. Going in and out of the dugout they were throwing watermelon rinds at me, orange peels, peanuts, garbage, just about anything they could get their hands on.

The black umpire behind the plate finally called time. He said, "I'm going to put a stop to this shit." I'm crying on the mound. I'm literally wiping my eyes and throwing the ball up to the plate with tears on it.

The umpire went over to their dugout and told them, "I hear that word one more goddamn time and I'm going to clear the fucking dugout. As a matter of fact, you better come up here swinging because everything he throws is a strike." That's what he told them; I was standing right there.

Then, going back to the dugout, I got hit in the face with a banana peel. Of course they weren't going to find out who threw it. I was upset, but I went out and continued to pitch. I even finished the game. Fifteen strikeouts, two hits, one run. I remember I punched out the last batter and all the guys came running to the mound.

But we had to hurry up and get out of there. The crowd was hot, and so all my teammates ganged around me and we got to the bus. They threw some rocks and stuff at the bus, screamed obscenities, that type thing. We didn't say anything back. We'd won 12–1; we'd said all we had to say on the field.

• • •

1977 was my senior year and Coach Marchant took a job in Texarkana, Arkansas. I guess he got more money or whatever, but he had done his time. He won some championships and made himself a very famous high school baseball coach in our area. As of 2012 he's with the Delta State athletic department. He was the baseball coach there, even after he had an unfortunate accident in his Jeep that left him partially paralyzed.

When Coach Marchant left, a black coach by the name of Bill McFarland—"Coach Mac" we called him—who I'd had since I was in the seventh grade, took over. He had worked under Coach Marchant for about five or six years as his assistant coach. He understood the game, but he didn't know it like Coach Marchant, so he would ask for assistance from me and Rush Davis and some other seniors on the team. How to set up the practices, fielding and hitting and bunting drills, all the things that Coach Marchant had written out, we had to take charge of it now.

I went to a 4-A high school. Those were the major sports schools in Mississippi. Three or four guys were getting drafted off our high school team. It was the best baseball, possibly, in the state of Mississippi. There were a few other schools around that were pretty good, right around our level. That was the year that I showed that I had promise, that I could become a pretty decent baseball player, a pretty decent pitcher.

Hopes were high that year for this senior we had, Rush Davis. "Rush this, Rush that," everywhere you went. Now, I don't take anything away from Rush, but while he was supposed to be the stud on the team, I showed that I was every bit as good a pitcher as he was, and maybe better. Rush played on the high school All-Star team and was drafted straight out of high school in '77 by the Kansas City Royals. He got maybe as high as Triple A in the Cardinals organization after moving around a bit. He got drafted—partially on size, I think—and at the time he was throwing maybe 90 or 91 mph. Not a blazing fastball, but a little bit better fastball than I had. A couple years later I maxed out at 94 or 95 mph. I was a small kid in high school. Rush must have been 215 pounds as a senior, while I was only about 142 pounds.

He was the ace and I was behind him on the staff. I didn't like playing second fiddle because I felt that I'd showed that I had just as much promise as him. Rush getting selected for the high school All-Star game, I envied that quite a bit. I was quite upset because they had chosen two more pitchers in the state of Mississippi from the local area over me as well. I was better than these guys and I knew I was. Believe me, the future told it—I went to the major leagues and they didn't go nowhere. That's the whole story.

But at the same time, that was the year I was offered a few scholarships. I chose the scholarship to go to Jackson State University, which was a great choice. I had a chance to go to some other schools and some bigger schools, but I chose to go to school right down the highway. I found out that they had a great program, they had a history of a lot of ballplayers being drafted, and an outstanding coach in Robert Braddy.

He brought me in there. He wanted my brothers, too, before me, but they signed out of high school. My brother Neal didn't get drafted out of high school either, but he went on to Tuskegee. He's a year and a half older than I am and so I was thinking about going to Tuskegee as well, but Neal talked me out of it. I guess he and the coach had a falling out down there. Neal didn't bring me into the program, and apparently he said that if Neal didn't bring *me* into the program then he didn't want Neal. So Neal ended up transferring to Jackson State with me and turned out to be one of the best ballplayers that Coach brought in.

Neal sat out '78 as a transfer, but he came back in '79—my sophomore year—and was our starting right fielder. He hit first, second, and third in the lineup, while compiling a .300 batting average. He was a real good ballplayer. Neal should have been drafted, but for whatever reason, he wasn't. I still say my brother Mike's troubles had something to do with that.

I had great years at Jackson State. I was 20–5 in school. I'm in the school's Hall of Fame. There were other ballplayers who were ranked over me, but I did all the things I was supposed to do. In '79 I really figured it out. My freshman year I was 3–1, because I was timid. I was just turning 18, coming in there playing with big-time ballplayers, I was quite intimidated. But the next year I matured, and I knew I belonged.

◆ ◆ ◆

Growing up in the South, all of my friends had cool nicknames, names like Bra-dick, Dead Eye, and Popsicle. Along the way, pretty much everybody got a nickname, one way or another. Hell, even my mom had a nickname: Sweetie.

Ever since I was a little boy my mom would send me around to Big Mama's house to pick up her booze. Now, Big Mama was a bootlegger; she sold cheap rot-gut whiskey. I can still remember my mom instructing me on how to sneak the booze back home. "Pull your shirt over it so your daddy can't see it," she'd say. "Come in the back door and hide it under the kitchen cabinet."

I didn't know at the time that my mom was an alcoholic and that my dad didn't want her drinking that shit. She told me to hide it, so I did. But it wasn't too long until I was drinking it myself. From what I understand I was born an alcoholic, so it was inevitable.

Anyway, I was 17 years old in '77, getting ready to finish my senior year in high school. One of my best friends at that time was Pap. He was a distant cousin, but we were real close. Pap had been in trouble his whole life, in and out of reform school since he was eight or nine years old, basically for stealing. He couldn't keep his hands off shit.

So one day Pap and I were together, and this was around the time we started drinking a lot of cheap wine—really drinking anything we could get our hands on. I told Pap that I knew where Big Mama kept the corn whiskey. We broke into Big Mama's place and stole some whiskey. Then we took it down to a nearby tin shed to drink it. Now, on top of selling whiskey, Big Mama used to house all the drunks in the neighborhood, feeding them this rot-gut whiskey and stealing their social security checks. One of the local drunk homeless men was a guy called Mr. Fat Mama, and that day he happened by Pap and me and our looted liquor.

Mr. Fat Mama told Big Mama that Sweetie's baby, Dennis Ray, and Ms. Eloise's baby, Pap, were down in the tin shed, drinking the whiskey from the oil cans. So Big Mama called me up to the house the next day and she scolded me and told me that I shouldn't be drinking that shit—I was too young.

The next day I saw Pap and he called me "Oil Can." And every day after, that's what he called me.

This is also around the time that I went to Tuskegee University for orientation, because I thought I might be going to school there. My brother Neal was there at the time, along with a ballplayer named Harrison Lewis, who we grew up playing ball with. My older brothers taught Harrison the game and Harry, in turn, showed me a lot about the game as a little boy. Neal told me how the fans loved Harry at Tuskegee. Harrison's nickname was also "Oil Can," after the Mighty Mouse character "Oil Can Harry." Neal told me how the fans chanted, "Oil Can" when he would pitch. I thought that shit was so cool. Besides, I was a crazy Mighty Mouse fan.

So after going to orientation at Tuskegee I went back home to Meridian and got ready for my high school baseball season, at the same time playing intramural basketball with Pap and the gang. Pap was still calling me "Oil Can" and so I wrote "Oil Can" under the bill of my cap. Then my high school shortstop, Ricky Irby, picked up my ball glove and cap one day during spring practice and he saw the nickname in my cap. Every day after that Ricky started calling me "Oil Can," too.

That's how the name got from the streets to the baseball diamond. A few months later I was recruited to go to Jackson State, and when it came time to sign my scholarship the application asked if I had a nickname. I put "Oil Can," and the rest is history.

4: Cocaine

"I smoked crack in the
clubhouse in Oakland..."

4: Cocaine

M y troubles started in 1981.

That's when I really first learned about cocaine, was in Colombia in '81. A couple of us ballplayers were on vacation down there. I kept noticing this one lady out walking around the hotel, down by the beach, all the time in sundresses. She was a very flamboyant white lady; and one day I heard her speak. She was asking an employee something, and right away I realized that she ain't just from the States, she's from some place around where I'm from. So I got to talking with her and her husband, turns out they were from Memphis. He was a brilliant, rich guy who spoke like seven languages. Anyway, the two of them invited some of us up to their room, and when we got in there the whole damn table was full of cocaine.

I was naïve. I didn't really know anything about coke. I tried a little bit, we hung out a while, and then we left. Later I noticed that I didn't want to eat anything and I couldn't sleep. But I really didn't pay it much attention. I said, "I guess this is what this shit does."

Then I was back in the States, and it was like what I did down there I left down there. I went to spring training, then

59

THEY CALL ME OIL CAN

Boston, then out on the road, and I didn't ever see any coke. That was '82, the year I got called up, and I went the whole season doing what I always did: smoking pot every single day. But I never thought about—and nobody on the team ever talked about—any real drugs, any cocaine or anything. It wasn't around, and it was just something I tried once in my life, so it wasn't no thing.

I split the '83 season between Triple A and the big leagues. Then, in the off-season, I got a call from some old college teammates who were living in Chicago, so I went to stay with them for a while. We didn't know anything about drugs in college, but here it was three years later and we're in the big city. So I go out to a club with them one night and they got a little pile of cocaine. I snorted some, but then on the way home I started throwing up. That stuff messed me up. I did not like it. I didn't even think of it as an experiment. It was like I tried some food that I didn't like and so I wouldn't eat it anymore.

After Chicago I went back down to Mississippi, where I got together with Karen, my future wife. I'd met her in Pawtucket and she came to stay with me at my apartment in Jackson. One night, some of my friends from Meridian came over. We were just sitting up there playing cards or whatever, and one of them said, "Y'all ever did any cocaine?"

So some of us did a little bit together, and it wasn't so bad this time.

Then I'm gone. Winter Haven for spring training, and I make the team, and so it's on to Boston for the '84 season. I'm throwing the ball real good, and I got a nice place in the Granada Highlands in Malden, north of Boston, and I'm making friends and doing well. Everyone's being nice to me because I'm a celebrity. Someone offers a little coke here, a little coke there, this is when I started to experiment a little bit more with it. Nothing

60

too serious. I didn't have that much time to mess around, anyway. You play a game, you come home at night, and you have to get up and be at the ballpark the next day. I started to do a little bit, but I was functioning fine.

Then I got sent down. Ralph Houk and I got into an argument when he said something that I took to be racist, or at least racially insensitive, and so I got pissed as hell. He sent me down after four starts—four starts! He said something about me being undisciplined. Maybe that was the reason, or maybe it was because of that argument. We had the argument, and then after my next start I got sent down.

I wanted to play winter ball the year before and the Red Sox said no—Haywood Sullivan called me in and they knew I wanted to make money and they started paying me year-round, instead of just during the season.

So then it was after the '84 season, and I met this one guy and we started hanging out a bit. He lived up north, but he came down to Mississippi to visit. That was when I found out that this guy was the biggest cokehead I'd ever known.

We were hanging out at this hotel in Meridian, and I was snorting a little powder. But then this guy told me that he wanted some coke, too, but he wanted it *another way*. I didn't know what he was talking about. He said, "I want it cooked up."

"What're you talking about, you want it cooked up?"

He just assumed that I knew about it, but I told him I didn't. He said, "When you buy the powder, just tell whoever's selling it to you to cook it up. Just say that."

I went to the dope house and I said exactly what he said. So the guy came out and gave me some shit wrapped in aluminum foil. I opened it up and looked at it. I thought maybe that was how powder cocaine came before it was broken up. I didn't know.

When I got back to the hotel room he had me get him a soda can and an ashtray. I didn't know why, because he didn't smoke cigarettes. He acted like he had an important call, a private conversation, and he went in the bathroom. He kept going in and coming out—I'm in the room doing some lines and he's freebasing in the bathroom and I don't know what's going on. He poured out the soda—I know all this stuff now—and made a pipe out of the can, and he needed the ashtray for the ashes. But I didn't know any of that then. That's how naïve I was.

He stayed with me for three or four days. He had some friends in Memphis, which is only like three and a half hours from there, so we rode up to see them. I had my little Cutlass and I drove him.

We went to this other guy's apartment. I was in the living room and they were in the kitchen. This other guy, he's got water boiling on the stove, pots and tubes and shit laying around, like a chemist. I was just sitting there, snorting some powder, smoking a little weed. Then I smell this crazy aroma. I said. "What y'all doing over there. Is something burning?"

He called me over and said, "Hey, you want to try this?"

And I said, "Why not?"

So he gave it to me. As soon as I hit that pipe I ran to the bathroom and started throwing up. I could hear this guy laughing, hear the other guy saying, "Oh, he got young lungs, he's young." So I came out of there, and man I was feeling messed up.

We were driving back to Mississippi so he could catch a plane out of Jackson. He was still smoking as we went down the highway. He's breaking off pieces and smoking them, and I'm driving but he's real quiet over there. He'd talk a little bit every now and then but he seemed real tired. I noticed that his tie was loose and he was sweating. He kept telling me, "Don't speed, drive slow." It really hadn't even dawned on me that we were doing something illegal.

All of a sudden I realized that we're both high, I got some weed and some powder on me, and this guy's freebasing in the front seat. Now I was scared.

• • •

I almost missed my wedding. I got so fucked up the day of my wedding that I almost didn't make it. December 31, 1985. A friend of mine came by to see me and we went riding. I was getting married about four or five in the evening, and we just started getting high early that morning. We got high all day, all the way to up to the time I had to put on the tuxedo. I was so messed up that my friend had to dress me. I couldn't even put on my own tux.

When I got to Winter Haven in February I rode off into this little drug-infested area of town called the Boggy Bottom, where the Haitians and the Jamaicans lived. I was still young. I think that's the night that it all really started.

I'd smoked crack a few times, but I still hadn't gotten into that world completely. I had $50 to spend, figured I'd get a little half-gram and I'd go back to the house and get messed up. I got a guy there to hook me up, so I saw him and said, "Go get me some of this."

He said, "What you want?"

"I want to spend $50."

"No, just give me $20."

I said, "I'm not going to give you $20. Just take the whole $50 and bring me whatever that'll bring me." I didn't know what he was talking about. I know if you got a pile, half a gram of powder, it's $50. $100 for a gram, I'm just getting half a gram.

He came back with some shit about as long as my finger. He put it in my hand and I said, "What is *this*?" I didn't know what it was—because it wasn't round—but it was crack. It was flat. It was funny looking. "What do you do with this here?"

He said, "You *smoke* it." And he handed me a car antenna, broke and bent, with a Brillo Pad inside it. "Let me get in the car," he said as he climbed in the back seat. He turned the light on so he could see what he was doing. "Give me a piece of that." I gave him the whole thing and he broke off a piece. He measured it, broke off a little piece, and started smoking.

I said, "Let me try that," and I've been fucked up ever since.

I went home and smoked. We noticed it was a funny kind of high, not like powder high. All I wanted was some more. So I went and found the guy again—that same night—and I said, "Get me some more of that."

This time I gave him $300 and told him to get me as much as he could with that. He came back with a handful of rock. I didn't really know if you could have a heart attack and die from it. I didn't know about none of that. All I knew was that I was going to smoke it.

Man, I found myself going down there every damn day, and all I'm thinking is, *I like this.* I didn't know I was getting hooked. I'm just thinking I like it, like going to the ice cream parlor, or like your favorite cookie—but more than that, like it's the best pussy in the world or something. I like it. That's all I know.

After practice I'm gonna go get some of that. Every fucking day.

• • •

Eventually, some folks started to notice that I was losing weight. I'd always been skinny, but by the time spring training started and everybody showed up, people were like, "Damn, what's wrong with Can?" I didn't even know. I looked in the mirror and thought I looked normal. I hadn't even realized that I was down to 125 pounds.

I was working out every day, throwing and running and everything, and when I'd get through working out I'd go eat at Mrs. C's Soul Food. Then I'd walk right out her back door, down the alley, and score. Right out of the restaurant, all the crack in the world. My food didn't even get a chance to digest before I was smoking. Then I smoked all day and night until the next day. I just went home and hid—I didn't even know I was killing myself. I didn't know until this one day at spring training when Marty Barrett's wife, Robin, pulled me over to the side and said, "Something ain't right with you. You haven't been eating and something isn't right. You don't look good."

I remember I was kind of embarrassed.

Late in spring training Dr. Pappas called me into the office and asked me what was going on. He said, "You messing with drugs?"

I said, "Doc, I smoke some weed and tried a little cocaine."

"You *tried* a little cocaine? How did you try it?"

"I snorted it."

He said, "You didn't smoke it?"

"Well...yeah."

"Shit! How often?"

"Every day," I said.

"Every day?"

"Every day."

He said he wanted to run some tests on me, because my eyes were yellow and I wasn't looking good. He told the media that I had noncontagious viral hepatitis. Then he sent me off to Boston to get me cleaned up.

I had the whole cover story about hepatitis, but it was flat-out me smoking crack every damn day. I was smoking cocaine, freebasing, doing crack; they had all kind of names for it back then. But whatever you call it, that's what I was doing.

So here it was, 1986, and when I got back I was ready to play. I was starting to get my weight back, learning about the drug and all that, but I still hadn't admitted to myself that I was hooked or anything. But I did know one thing: that dope was always on my mind. It was starting to talk to me like a person. "Hey, I'm down here. This is cocaine. Come get me."

"No shit? I'll be right there."

• • •

I first met Dr. Arthur Pappas in '82, when I came to the big leagues. I shortly learned that he was not only the team doctor, he was also a part owner of the Red Sox. That always seemed to me like a conflict of interest.

That kind of pertained to me in '86, when I was having my problems with cocaine. That whole thing changed the way I was perceived by the organization. They thought they could treat me differently since I had indulged in drugs. It was something they could use against me because of my open, natural personality. But what they really feared the most was me knowing who I was, which was a strong, independent African American.

So it was a thing where, at the same time that they were trying to come to my rescue, it was also something they used against me. With other ballplayers, they would be like, "Ah, he's got a problem, we have to help him." With me it was more like, "We knew he was going to go down that road. This is what we expected." If I'd have been more status quo or if I had not been so outspoken, I probably would have gotten more sympathy. I felt like I was on warning already with my personality being like it was, and then all of a sudden they found out I had a drug problem, and I think that gave them the freedom to treat me a certain way.

I was never a kid to think about my worth or my value to the team. It was irrelevant for me to think about it like other ballplayers did, because I just loved playing the game, so I didn't think about the money. I didn't think about things like how the organization viewed my value.

In '86, though, I started to understand that stuff. I thought they were helping me when they turned my drug problem into hepatitis, but then I realized that they were helping themselves, too. That's when I first encountered that part of why the team helps you is because you're part of their property. So maybe they hide that you had some kind of drug problem or drinking problem—which they did for several other ballplayers—but they're doing it to protect their investment as much as they are to help you. And then, at the same time, me having the personality that I had made the media attack it in a different way. I wasn't a quiet athlete. I was a very noticeable and outgoing player, so the public and the fans wanted to know about my life. At times that was a curse, and at others it's been a blessing.

After the hospital I was healthy enough to open up the season. The drug problem was still there but I had a better handle on it, and I was starting to understand what I was dealing with. I wasn't just lying there in the hospital, I was being counseled about what I'd been doing and how dangerous it was.

The Red Sox were concerned about me stopping. Dr. Pappas, throughout the season, kept an eye on me. Even the last part of spring training, after I came back, he had a person live in my house with me. He had the trainer, Charlie Moss, come by and check on me every day after I left the ballpark. They did everything but drug test me.

I told them I'd get a handle on it, and for the most part I did. Throughout the '86 season I did pretty well. There was a day out here and there, a few bad nights on the road, a few bad ones at home, that type of thing. In spurts it would get out of control. I wasn't doing it every day, but on the days I did it, hell I did it for 12 hours straight.

They called me in and told me if I didn't stop they were going to put me in rehab. I said, "Nah, hell no, I ain't going to no rehab." This was around the All-Star break, when I was pitching real well. I'm not *living* like I should, but I'm pitching like hell. And I'm pitching under this stress, knowing that I have these two lives I'm living. I'm a prowler running the street at night, sleeping it off during the day, then I'm a major league pitcher at the ballpark. All my teammates, at one time or another, came to me and said, "Get your rest tonight." At least one of them, every day. I was concentrating and maintaining, because I knew I had to pitch well with me living like I was living.

The articles I was reading in the papers were rough, though. The articles meant that my teammates were talking bad about me. I mean, it's not coming from the writer, because the writer doesn't know me. So I could tell that they were asking other people and other people were giving their opinions.

I remember most vividly crying to Dr. Pappas one day and telling him that I felt that some of my teammates were making it out like I was a bad teammate because I got on some dope. He told me, "That's not true. They know you're a very sweet person, they know that you're a kind person." But I told him I was hearing certain things. Some of the players that I was close with would come to me and say that when they were in the outfield shagging balls this guy said this and this guy said that.

I knew who some of these people were who were talking about me. They liked seeing me down, because it gave them a chance to put me down and make them feel like it was bringing them up. They were envious of me and of the type of person that I was, but now they could be like, "Look at me, I'm not on drugs. Look at him, he is. Now, maybe I can't out-pitch him but I'm clean. I can't out-play him but I'm clean. I'm a better person."

That attitude is what managers took to keep me out of the All-Star Game.

This is the type of shit that I was going through.

Some guys were talking to me just to basically try and check what kind of mood I was in, so they could run back and say, "He's high right now," or "He's not high today." Not that they cared. I was getting a lot of mixed feelings.

That particular year really made me famous—made me infamous, too. That's why people know me. People knew I was colorful and a good ballplayer. Even the negativity I got eventually turned into a positive. I never complained or talked about it in public. (In fact, I never really talked about my life like this until right now.)

I only opened up behind closed doors. I'd talk with Dr. Pappas, and he'd let me express my emotions and the way I saw life. I'm sure he hadn't ever talked to an African American ballplayer like he did with me. I was trying to express to him how I felt about being an African American. He just didn't know. He didn't know I had a nephew I'd never seen; he didn't know our church got burned down; he didn't know about the Klan threatening Michael because of his half-white babies.

I didn't even talk about this stuff with the black ballplayers I was friends with. Guys like Ellis Burks or Chico Walker or Sam Horn. I didn't talk to them about those type things. The only ballplayer who maybe knows is Delino DeShields, my teammate in Montreal, because he spent more personal time with me than any of those guys. He's been to my home and met my family.

Marquis Grissom can relate because he grew up in the same type of household, same type of family background; it was very similar to my life.

But it was Dr. Pappas who I felt most comfortable talking to. The descendent of a slave from Mississippi, and the man I opened up to was a Greek man who owned the ballclub I worked for. They were pretty unique conversations. He was almost like a father figure to me at that time.

• • •

In the off-season, after the '86 season, Dr. Pappas had my college coach come by to check on me. He requested I go back to school and take some classes, get focused, do some different things in the off-season. It felt funnier than hell to be sitting up there in the classroom with those kids. It was a weird feeling to walk on the Jackson State campus. I was walking down the sidewalk, and one of the frat boys recognized me, so he sent the pledges over and made them bow and pledge to me. I could hear students saying, "Who the hell is *that*?"

"He just pitched in the World Series, man."

School was basically my rehab. Taking classes helped me stay focused. See, I wasn't going to talk to a doctor, no damn way! It wasn't that I couldn't admit that I had a problem, I just wasn't going to talk to anybody about it. Nobody would understand. Hell, I'm still like that. That's why I can't go on *Celebrity Rehab*. I'm not Dwight Gooden; I don't want to sit up there and talk to you about my life in front of the whole world. I'll deal with it.

I just took it one day at a time.

• • •

I smoked crack in the clubhouse in Oakland, but only after a close call on the ballfield. I had brought the rocks with me from Boston on a charter, but then when I was out there on the mound I started to get paranoid. I wasn't scared that they'd know I was on it, I was just all of a sudden sure that they'd find it. It was in my locker, and then it was like it was all I could think about. "Damn, they're going to search my locker and find it."

So I went in the clubhouse, got the crack, and put it under the lining of my baseball cap. Rocks. In my hat! I'm out there pitching in the game, and if you remember, when I pitched my hat would sometimes come off my head. I didn't wear it down on my head. I had it sitting up on my head. So, of course, what happens? I fired this one pitch and my hat flew off. I looked down at the mound and there were rocks all over. I picked up a couple of rocks, like I'm cleaning the mound, like I got gravel or something on the mound. I'm picking it up, putting what I can in my pocket, cleaning that stuff off. I even mashed a couple of them into the dirt, ground them into the mound with my foot.

Then I just went on pitching and won the game.

I knew where to find it in every city I went to. It was easy to find. All you had to do was tell the bell captain or the cab driver. Some cities, some nights were worse than other ones. Usually, you misbehave more at home, just because you're at home and you know where everything is. On the road I tried to get my rest a little bit more.

The thing about it is that in every city I played in I knew somebody. I knew a relative, or somebody I went to college with, or somebody I grew up in Meridian with, who had moved to San Francisco or Seattle or wherever. Chicago was a rough place for me because two-thirds of my college teammates were from Chicago. We were just young and partying, and here it is today, and some of them are addicts like hell. Some of them are dead, and I'm stuck with it.

Dwight Gooden and I talked about how we both knew that when it got to be a certain time of night we had to go. It was a phobia we both had. When it started getting late and you started drinking, take your ass home or you're going to end up at a crack house at two or three in the morning.

But I didn't have anyone with me, so I had to watch myself on the road. We're all kind of by ourselves. You know, I know some of my teammates were smoking crack, too, but not one ever talked to me about it or offered me any. Teammates offered me some powder when I first came into the game, but when I learned to freebase cocaine it became a secretive thing for me. It was something I learned to hide. The attitude was: I know you get high and you know I get high, but we don't get high together, so I can't tell what you did and you can't tell what I did. It ain't that I don't trust you. It ain't that you don't trust me. It's just almost like a defensive respect or some type of thing. I can look at you and tell that you stayed up all night—and I know I did, too—but we weren't together, so we don't have to look at each other like users or addicts. We can still see each other just as ballplayers.

It's addict behavior.

Only another addict on the team can tell you what I'm saying and feel what I'm feeling. Once I was on the bus or driving to the ballpark, I couldn't wait to eat and just hang out. I couldn't wait to get to the ballpark, because at the hotel I hadn't eaten because I was getting high. So when I got to the ballpark I'd get something to eat, then I'd get undressed and go take a shower. All the guys who get high know what you're up to. Other guys didn't know. They were naïve. Some guys knew what I was doing because they'd been there, too. They'd come to me and say, "I know what you're doing." They knew your behavior, but they also protected you.

They'd say, "Get some rest tonight," because they knew I didn't get any the night before. They knew me. They knew that if I ain't talking on the bench and bullshitting around and basically just the craziest guy in the dugout, then something's wrong with me. There's a difference between a weed high and a high that lets you know, "Don't bother me." Nobody ever knew when I was high on weed, because I wasn't ever not high on weed.

A reporter once asked me how many games I pitched when I wasn't high on weed.

None.

Well, I started a few without smoking up, but I didn't like it. I'd be warming up in the bullpen and I could hear the fans and the vendors and the damn drink machines, and it's distracting.

I smoked during games. I've gone out into my car, during the game, and smoked weed or crack. And this is in the parking lot at Fenway. In between innings I'd go through the back door, out to my car in the garage, smoke up, and then run back into the clubhouse. A few times I was almost late getting to the mound because I was running back down the runway. "I had to use the restroom," I'd say, but I'd been out in the parking lot.

But that's how so many of us were back then. Tim Raines told me a story once. He said he slid into stole second base and when he slid a vial fell out onto the ground. He said the umpire looked at it and said, "What the fuck?" and before he could see what it was Tim picked it up and stole third on the next pitch. He's gone. Then there's a base hit and he crosses home and just keeps on running, right into the clubhouse so he can hide it.

• • •

I still have a problem with cocaine today. I don't look at how long I been off it or anything, I just maintain and go a day at a time. I got a control now—in the last eight years or so—that I never had. I've been using since '81, so you're talking about 30 years, on and off.

When they say, "You been clean six months," or, "Oh man, you been off it a year," that doesn't mean a thing. That don't matter, man. I've been off for three years and it came back overnight. I know guys who have been off it for 20 years, but they're hooked on it now.

So it's funny to me when people ask, "How long you been clean?" like it matters. There's some folks out there that can say, "I *was* clean for 20 years but I'm back on it now." How does that sound?

It's the strangest thing in the world. It's something I fight every day. I don't deny it. I don't say nothing to nobody, I just take care of myself. I just make sure I get home to my family every night. I try not to be in places or around people that are into it; I try not to be around that atmosphere. It's about me.

5: Still Fighting

"I didn't care if I ever toed

the rubber again."

Still Fighting

A lot of stuff started to go wrong when I was passed over for the All-Star team in 1986. Sparky Anderson didn't pick me in '85, and I was already real upset about that. Then '86 came around and I was pitching better than anyone. I was an All-Star, no doubt about that, but Dick Howser didn't pick me.

I didn't care about the bonus; I just wanted to play. I didn't care if they paid me, not one dime, but I wanted to be where the best were. I'm part of the elite group of people who play this game. That's what the All-Star team means to me. It was more personal—a slight on me—than anything that I would ever experience in the game.

The year before, in '85, Lloyd Moseby endorsed me and said, "It should be Oil and Gas"—meaning me and Doc Gooden—going against each other. Lloyd Moseby said it would be the best All-Star Game in the history of All-Star Games to watch Doc and me pitch against each other. Two black pitchers going up against each other—one real colorful and the other one throwing gas? Man, people would be tearing the TV apart trying to get to it. And they made sure it wasn't going to happen.

Then in '86, I said, "Well, Doc went. Hell, I'm going." There's no way they can pass me over again.

When I didn't get picked in '86, it was the reporters in the clubhouse who told me. We had just come off the field. It shocked me when they told me, because at the time I wasn't even thinking about the All-Star team. You know why I wasn't thinking about it? In my mind and in my soul I was in. I just knew I was on the All-Star team. Clemens and me, we're both shoe-ins. I'm going right behind him. I was 10–5, and the stats showed I should have been 13–3. Roger was 14—0 and I could have won 13.

The reporters came to my locker. I remember all these reporters standing around, and the looks in their eyes when I got upset. I heard what they said and I turned and said, "Motherfucker didn't do *what*?" Then I just went off. I started saying all kinds of crazy stuff and started taking off my uniform. I was walking to the shower and I just said, "I don't want to play this shit no more. I'm through with this shit. I don't want to play. Y'all can have the uniform, I'm going to shower, and I'm going home."

Then the trainer stuck his head in the shower and says, "Dr. Pappas wants to see you."

I said, "Fuck Dr. Pappas! I don't want to talk to nobody—I don't care who wants to see me, I'm out of here. As a matter of fact, go tell that son of a bitch that didn't pick me that he's a redneck bigoted motherfucker."

So I went and got my clothes, and the press was still trying to talk to me. They knew I was mad about it and now they wanted to get a reaction, so I got angrier. I yelled, "I'm not saying anymore. Don't ask me about any shit now."

Then I just walked out. I got in my car, turned to the parking attendant—and I'll never forget this because he still teases me about it today when he sees me—and I said, "Al, I'm out of this here. I quit.

"Where're you going?"

"I'm going home."

When I got home I just locked myself away. I didn't even call down to Mississippi for a day or two, didn't talk to my parents or anything. The Red Sox sent somebody to my house and I told them to go away. They were asking me to come back. "They want you to come back."

I told them, "I ain't never coming back. As a matter of fact, I'm in here packing to go to Mississippi right now."

They tried to get Don Baylor to talk to me. I wouldn't talk to him either. I called him an "Uncle Tom bastard." I said, "Why'd they send you to talk me? They think I'll talk to you because you're black?"

"Oh Can, come on."

"I ain't hearing that shit. Goddamnit, I can out-pitch God. They ain't going to let me play, then I'm done."

They made sure I didn't go anywhere, though. I noticed that the police stayed right there outside my door. And when I say outside, I mean on my porch! I looked out the door and there were cops sitting on my steps. They were going to stay there until I came back to the ballpark. A reporter from the *Herald* came by and I threw my drink at him, and those cops just sat by, watching.

How did it end? Dr. Pappas called and got in touch with my father-in-law. They'd met a few times and they had kind of got close. So my wife's dad drove up to my house and he said, "Dr. Pappas has been trying to get in touch with you." He said that I needed to go back to the ballpark and apologize for the outburst and all that. And for a couple of days I wouldn't do it. I wasn't going back and apologizing. No way. I didn't care about anything just then. I didn't care about the team, didn't care about winning, didn't care about anything other than the fact that they'd passed me over. I didn't even care about pitching no more once I didn't get picked for the All-Star team. I didn't care if I ever toed the rubber again. That was the end of my career, that night, that was the end of it, and it didn't wake up until I got to Montreal.

• • •

Eventually I did go back, but since I hadn't done like they asked they suspended me for 21 days. I was at home when the All-Star break came. It was the morning of the 16th or 17th of July, I think, and I went to get some cocaine at this grocery store where I knew some of the Colombians. I went into this grocery store, but as soon as I got there I noticed two narcs walk in. They were easy to spot, no matter how they dressed. White dudes, just too conservative to be in the 'hood.

So I left the store without buying anything and walked back to my car. When I got to my car, a Colombian was sitting in there. The door had been open and the dude just jumped in the car and told me to leave and leave now. "The police watching you. Leave now, you go home. You want something, we get it for you later. I send somebody by your house later." They all knew me. They were all big baseball fans and they protected me.

So this guy got out of the car and I left. I was headed back to the house, I looked in my rearview mirror and I saw this cop speeding behind me, up the hill and under the Tobin Bridge. I didn't have anything on me, so I wasn't too worried. They must have thought that I purchased some when that guy got in the car with me.

I pulled in the driveway and got out of the car, and before I was to the door they whipped in right behind me. One cop jumped out of the passenger side and said, "Get up against the car."

80

I said, "For what?"

"Get up against the car."

"Am I under arrest?"

Then he grabbed me and I pushed him off. I kept asking if I was under arrest and what for, but they wouldn't say. Then the other cop was out and grabbing at me, too.

I had a houseguest staying with me at the time, and he came running out and just saw two dudes grabbing me, so he pulled one off, and then they started tussling. They're thinking my houseguest is a dealer, and the one cop pulls his piece and is getting ready to shoot him. Now, the property that I lived on was a private neighborhood, so they had their own security. So the security came up there and tried to calm everyone down and get the cops to leave us alone. Then a whole bunch of cops showed up and they grabbed hold of both of us.

A bunch of the neighbors were out, watching it all go down. One of my neighbors was a lawyer, and said to me, "I saw everything they did. Mr. Boyd. If you need me to represent you, I will." He was a white guy, and he said, "I heard you ask whether you were under arrest and I saw him aggressively come at you, and he didn't say anything when you asked him if you were under arrest."

Now all these cops had a hold of me, and I can hear them saying stuff like, "Man, he has to be on *something*. There ain't no man this size that strong." They were trying to get my hands behind my back, pulling harder and harder—and I'm screaming at them that my arm is my livelihood, and they just wrenched it back as hard as they could.

They kept working at it until the security *made* them stop. Security told them, "You need to get away from him right now. If he isn't under arrest then everybody [move away]." Everything sort of calmed down after that, and when they saw that I didn't have anything on me and that they had nothing to arrest me for, they left.

My father-in-law found me a lawyer, and he straightened all the stuff out, both with the cops and the Red Sox. The lawyer got them to drop everything. I didn't have any drugs on me, and it wasn't resisting arrest because the officer never said I was under arrest, plus they couldn't get me for assault charges, because there was no reason for them to touch me in the first place.

The lawyer wanted to sue them for what they'd done, but I just told him, "No, I just want to pitch."

When I came back I was in an arm brace, but Dr. Pappas told me to take it off. I said, "Why am I going to take it off? They hurt my arm. My arm ain't feeling good and I want some x-rays."

I felt like he was trying to make it seem like I was making it up, but I told him, "Doc, you weren't there. I had to tussle and fight people off me." He got mad, because I didn't want to take the arm brace off. He thought I was lucky, because they didn't catch me with nothing. I said, "I'm not lucky."

He got all upset about it. "Let me take the brace off."

Two days later I went out to play catch and I felt this twinge in my arm. "Man, this don't feel right." A few days later, I go back and I play some more catch and the twinge is kind of going away. I had a bullpen session before my next start, and I noticed something in my velocity. The ball just wasn't coming out as firm. There was this little funny feeling in there. Still, I did my job and pitched the rest of the season. I threw the clincher, with Billy Buckner catching the pop fly to end the game. I threw against the Angels in the ALCS; all the way to the World Series, all of it.

Every other day, my arm wouldn't feel good. I was stretching it and everything, but all the while I'm saying to myself, "These guys really did hurt my arm."

• • •

The '86 World Series was rough for me. I remember I went to pick up my family at the airport on the day of Game 3 and my dad had brought his wife with him. The family didn't get along with my stepmom or her family. Even today, we've sworn that since my mom and dad are dead we'll never speak to our stepmom and stepsisters ever again. That's how messed up it is.

Plus, I had stayed up all night smoking cocaine. So I was double upset and irritable. When I got to the airport, there was my oldest brother. I had just talked to him the day before and he told me Dad wanted to come. I said, "Yeah, bring Dad and Mom, everybody else can come, Steve and any of my brothers and sisters. Bring them. I'll pay for the tickets, I'll pay for the flight. I'll do everything." But I specifically told him not to bring Daddy's goddamn wife.

They came to the ballpark—my mom, my oldest brother, my dad and my stepmom—and it was messing me up so bad to see tears in my mom's eyes. I was so upset with my daddy and my oldest brother—I couldn't even concentrate enough to warm up in the bullpen.

That messed me up. I started off the game upset, and then I got madder than hell after the first inning when the Mets scored four runs. That Lenny Dykstra kind of caught me off guard.

I didn't really know Lenny Dykstra, had never seen Lenny Dykstra. I didn't know he was a little toy cannon. I didn't know that he had that kind of pop in his bat, but believe me throughout my career I found out. He got three more bombs off of me. He kind of shocked me, and believe it or not, he hit a real good slider. The same slider that I'd thrown to a lot of lefties and they didn't touch it, or they hit it foul or hit it off their foot. I still don't know today how he kept it fair down and in like that. I watched the tape. It's an incredible swing. It's a swing that I ain't really seen anybody else put on a slider down and in. The ball's at your front foot and you keep it fair? At your back foot you can kind of keep it fair, but at your front foot you're going to hit it out front, foul. I still don't know how he kept it fair. It was the third pitch I threw him. I want to say I had a strike and a ball on him and went to throw a slider. Then we botched up a play in the infield and they finished the first inning with four runs.

Things settled down after that though, and I started pitching real well. I pitched five scoreless innings and then gave up two runs in the seventh. I tried to keep it there and give the team a chance to score some runs and get back in the ballgame, but you have to give credit to Bobby Ojeda. He pitched really well. He held us down.

I was definitely ready to pitch again. I wanted to win. It was a redemption type thing. I was 1–1 in the playoffs—losing Game 3 and winning Game 6 against the Angels—and 0–1 in the World Series, but I should've had another chance to pitch, in Game 7.

Everybody wanted to remember the whole roller coaster ride and the whole police scandal and all that, but Game 3 was my chance to go out there and do my thing.

But the thing was, I've always noticed that any team that beat me the first time never beat me the second time. It was a reporter who first brought it to my attention. That's even during the regular season. If I faced someone and they beat me the first time, the second time I beat them.

But like I said, I didn't get to pitch because McNamara says I was drunk, or because someone else said I was high. There was a lot of lying going on at that time. For instance, what McNamara said about Roger asking to come out of Game 6, that's not true either. Roger never opted to come out of the ballgame. Nowhere did he show or say, "Here, take the ball," and walk off the mound.

No, he did not. John McNamara asked for the baseball and Roger didn't want to give it to him. But he had to give it to him. He asked for the ball. He's the manager and when he asks for the ball, you have to give it to him.

The thing is, I have mixed feelings about McNamara, because I really care for the man. The man was really good with me. He even helped me get to Montreal. I just feel like he didn't do the right thing. He's 80 years old. He shouldn't be leaving here with that lie. He doesn't owe these people that don't like me nothing, so how can he let them push him into saying that shit, because he knows that it ain't true?

I heard what he said about Stapleton and that's not true, either. He said Stapleton's nickname was "Shaky." Well, I ain't ever heard it. David's got good hands. Now, he wasn't the greatest athlete, but he was very durable at third, second, short, and first. He was a good utility man, and he could hit. Why would McNamara say that? Why would he use these reasons for him not being a good manager? For poor managing?

That's just my point of view. They didn't want to eat crow and let me go out there. They'd rather lose the World Series, they'd rather take a chance, saying that Bruce was hot. I don't give a damn. Bruce would tell you right now that I would have won that ballgame. I was a better pitcher than he was. I didn't pitch behind him in the rotation; he pitched behind me.

And then some people said that I was drinking champagne in the clubhouse before the game was over. Somebody find somewhere on the tape where I was drinking champagne. Whoever said that is lying. I didn't open any champagne—matter of fact, when I went up in the clubhouse and saw this plastic and all up around the clubhouse I thought it was premature. I was like, "Why is this here?" To me, I'm a Southern man, this is a jinx. You don't put out champagne, you don't print up T-shirts, you don't do none of that. Someone's going to say they looked over and saw Oil Can celebrating. Celebrating what?

I was in the tunnel when that ball went through Bill Buckner's legs. I wasn't sitting on the bench, and I sure as hell wasn't in the clubhouse pouring back champagne. I was smoking a cigarette in the tunnel. I was standing right there behind everybody, nervous and smoking. I was pacing in the tunnel, and I was like, "Damn, man, get this guy out." I'm practically eating the cigarette back there. I heard the excitement. I heard the "Ohhhhhhhhhhhhhh." I heard the bottom drop and a big-ass cheer and what I saw...I saw Bill Buckner walking back across the field when I came out. I didn't even see the play happen, and it was almost too embarrassing to ask what happened.

I have to say though, I understood that if I wasn't going to pitch that night that Bruce Hurst would be the person that I would take a back seat to. Lefty had pitched well against the Mets, but I was prepared to pitch even better. When everything's on the line, that's when I would call on my best, and my best never failed me, regardless of being high or not.

• • •

So here it was, after the World Series, my wife is pregnant with my son Dennis. We went back to Jackson and I took some classes. Dr. Pappas wanted me to continue to go back to school to help me keep clean in the off-season, so that's what I did.

The Red Sox had me taking drug tests that off-season. They asked me if I had anyone I really trusted and I told them that I trusted my college coach. So Coach would come by the house administer the tests. He'd say, "Dennis, if you ain't clean I ain't going to give it to you. I ain't turning this shit into them people. If you're shit ain't clean, I ain't turning it in."

I said, "Coach, I'm fine." I gave it to them for two months straight. I took about 16 drug tests in the off-season, and I passed them all.

I was working out that off-season with Ike Golden, who had caught me in college. He'd signed with the White Sox in '80, but was living back home. Ike was playing catch with me in front of his apartment complex, and I could feel that I didn't want to get on top of the ball. I was throwing three-quarters and my wife said to him, "You see anything different than what you saw in college?"

He said, "Yeah, he's not throwing the ball overhand like he did."

But I didn't say anything to my wife, to the team, to anybody. I knew my arm was hurting. I'd felt it since that altercation with the cops.

Later that winter, in January, Karen and I went on a cruise with some of my Red Sox teammates. We were playing softball on one of the islands where we stopped. I was playing shortstop and Marty Barrett was playing second, and I picked the ball up and I threw it across the field, and Marty just turned and said to me, "You don't feel good, do ya?" I didn't say anything, just shrugged it off, but he knew.

"Your arm's hurt."

• • •

I threw the ball very well in spring training of '87. I didn't give up a run. The whole spring. I came into the '87 season looking for redemption. The past year had gone all to hell, some due to other peoples' faults and some my own. I was tired of being passed over and '87 was the year I was going to set it right.

I opened the season on the DL though. My arm was hurting and I told Charlie Moss and Dr. Pappas and they shrugged it off. I honestly feel that my run-in with the police the previous year had lingered. But every time I'd go out there it was, "Ah, just ice it down, might be a little tendonitis or whatever." I got about five or six cortisone shots in the shoulder. I found out later that this could have made my shoulder pretty much glass, getting so many shots in there. Nobody cared. Cortisone—two, three days in a row—so I could go out and pitch.

I pitched like that through April, May, June, and July. They waited until August before they gave me the surgery. Turns out when the police pulled my arm behind my back and over my head I got a hairline fracture. The fracture was small. That's why it would feel good sometimes and hurt others. They shot the dye in it the first time and it didn't show up. These fools thought I was faking, because it didn't show up. I said, "Man, my arm is *killing* me." They just kept running me out there to throw a bullpen the next day. I think Dr. Pappas was trying to please the Red Sox, and maybe thinking that I'm just mad because of the last year; I'm pouting. I said, "I ain't pouting, I'm hurt. Ain't nobody out here can out-pitch me—Hurst, Roger, nobody. And don't nobody want to pitch more than me. I'm hurt."

I pitched through pain and was afraid to say I was hurt because the media would eat it up. I knew I was hurt, but I didn't tell anybody. I came to win 20 that year. I wanted to prove that I shouldn't have been passed up.

Roger and Bruce pitched well that year. We were destined to go back to the Series, but I couldn't pitch and without me there just wasn't enough.

I was treated like crap that year. People were saying I wasn't a team player, that I didn't go to the park every day and stuff like that. If I can't pitch, why do I need to be at the ballpark?

They waited five months to give me the surgery, so I missed the whole season. I didn't know what to expect. I didn't know if my arm would come back like it was or not.

Mine didn't.

Then, in '88, I developed blood clots. I was able to start 23 games in '88 and only 10 in '89. I think I developed the blood clots from the injections and surgery in '87. And all of this from the altercation with the police in '86!

• • •

I signed with Montreal before the 1990 season, and it was the best time that I ever had playing baseball.

I was like, "Damn, man, how could I have not been here my whole career?"

Someone once asked which guys were cool in the Expos clubhouse. My answer: "All of them."

It was weird. There weren't any cliques. Everybody hung out with everybody, everybody talked to everybody. Even on the bench, everybody joked with everybody. It was a whole different atmosphere for me. You didn't feel like a stranger there.

I was off cocaine then. That's not a coincidence. It has a lot to do with how you feel, and it plays on your emotions, and when I got to Montreal I just felt so good. From '87 to '91, I only indulged one time. I had one night out in a four-year period, and that was in December '89, before I signed a contract with the Expos that January. I felt so good about myself and everything, I didn't even go out intentionally and get high. It was a party. I was just home in Meridian over the Christmas holidays and went to this bar to hang out and see some of my friends. When the club closed, some little thug boys approached me. I knew these boys' families, uncles and cousins and stuff, and all of a sudden I heard myself saying, "Y'all got some of that shit on ya?"

"You want some?"

"Yeah."

I think I gave them like $40 that night and went on back to the room with it. For two years, I hadn't even looked at it. But here it was December and I was a free agent and I just went right back to it.

But things changed for the better after I signed with Montreal and started playing ball with those guys. Going to Montreal I got to play with Tim Raines, Tim Wallach, Marquis Grissom, Larry Walker, and Spike Owen. Owen had been my teammate in Boston, and he really endorsed me coming up there. Spike and I were pretty close in Boston, and we knew each other from the minor leagues as well. Spike made it very easy for me to come and play in Montreal. He told the guys what type of person I was, and he talked through all the other stuff that went on with me in Boston. That really opened doors.

Spike made it very easy to come in there and to become comfortable, while playing with great teammates. I loved Dave Martinez and Tom Foley and Andres Galarraga. They were class-act ballplayers. Mike Fitzgerald caught me pretty much every day up there, and he really complemented what I did well as a pitcher. He made it easy for me to go up against National League teams. Having someone behind the plate that can feel and think with you, that knows your stuff, it lets you work very independently.

It was a lot of fun playing in Montreal, one of the best seasons I've had in baseball. I'm thankful that I got to play up there, even though I did leave on a bad note. I was traded down to Texas, which I didn't like. To me, being traded was someone saying they didn't want you. I took it personally and I felt unwanted, especially with how well things had been going in Montreal. In '90, I started 31 games and had a 2.93 ERA. Halfway through the '91 season with Montreal I'd started 19 games and had a 3.52 ERA. Then I was traded, and it all went to hell. I went down to

Texas to finish out the season. I started 12 games and had a 6.68 ERA with the Rangers, and that was that.

I never touched a big-league mound again.

After the season ended, Karen and I drove home to Meridian from Texas. I remember it was my birthday, October 6, and I was driving and I just turned to her and said, "They ain't gonna let me play no more."

She said, "What do you mean, they ain't gonna let you play no more?"

"I can feel it. I've pitched my last game in the big leagues."

"You're too good of a ballplayer for them to do that."

"That ain't got nothing to do with it."

6: The End

"Anybody who has ever seen
Dennis Boyd knows that
he can pitch. I know he can
pitch—but he can't pitch
for me."

The End

Pittsburgh brought me in on a minor league contract at the beginning of the 1992 season. I had a problem with a couple of the pitching instructors there who'd already made up their minds about me before they ever even met me.

I threw the ball well, I did everything I had to do, but I ended up having to leave the organization later that year after burning up the uniform. These people treated me like crap. One of the pitching coaches came to me and told me that they weren't going to bring me to the major leagues, because they couldn't trust that I was finished with my bad habits.

Now, I'd been brought in on a Triple A contract to go to Buffalo. I understood the realities of that. But then they told me I was just going to be in extended spring training. After pitching 10 years in the major leagues, no one even invited me to a big-league camp.

I knew it was a banishment. I knew that I'd been blackballed out of the game of baseball. I could tell because of the circumstances and the way people were talking to me. Reporters would come to me and say things like, "Baseball, right now, is probably sick of you." They'd tell me that the owners and GMs and coaches were tired of all of the blowups and tantrums. But nobody ever understood why these blowups and tantrums came about. They just said, "Hey, that nigger's out of control." So it got passed around like that. Even when I went to another organization, that was the word on me.

They knew that I could pitch, but the bottom line was that they didn't give a fuck how well I could pitch. A coach actually said to me once, "Nigger, if you don't change, you ain't going to the fucking major leagues. And you'll never pitch again."

I ended up walking out of the Pirates organization and basically quitting baseball. I knew that I'd probably never play again.

• • •

My last chance came during spring training of '93. I'd been invited to Cleveland for a private tryout with the Indians. The general manager didn't even know, just the coaches. That's how secret it was.

The morning of the tryout they got me out of the bed at 6:00 AM and told me to sneak over to the ballpark. It wasn't even daylight yet. I snuck over to the ballpark. By the time I got through stretching and getting loose, George Kalafatis, my agent, was there. He was watching me along with the pitching coach, Rick Adair, and the manager, Mike Hargrove. The whole thing was very hush-hush.

I told them beforehand that I was a little bit nervous. I ran across the outfield to get stretched out and then threw some long-toss with George. When I was good and ready I climbed up the mound. I told Hargrove, "My stuff's good today."

Then I just reared back and started throwing. Now this is the honest to God truth, I ain't never in my life thrown the baseball like I threw the baseball that morning. At no time—not even when I was 19 years old and throwing 95 mph—had I ever thrown the ball this good.

Later that same day, Mike Hargrove called me in the office there in Winter Haven to meet with me. He said, "Look, I faced you your first major league game and you did not throw the baseball like that." Those were his exact words. He said, "That's the best I've ever seen you throw a baseball.

"If it was my choice and I was in control of this, you would be in my rotation. You wouldn't just be on my pitching staff, you'd be in my five-man rotation. But your personality is bigger than your right arm." That's exactly what he said. I shook his hand. There wasn't any more said. I didn't question it. I didn't say, "Who said it? Who thought that?" I didn't ask any of that. I just said, "I appreciate it. Thanks for the tryout, Mike."

The very next day there was an article in the newspaper. Mike and them had talked to the general manager, John Hart, about how well I threw the ball. Apparently, Hart told them that he didn't give a damn how well I threw the ball. He told the papers something like: anybody who has ever seen Dennis Boyd knows that he can pitch. I know he can pitch—but he can't pitch for me.

See, this stuff isn't really about my personality. My personality, as far as Major League Baseball is concerned, is that I'm an outspoken Negro. It's just like it was with Albert Belle. Albert was from Louisiana, and he just wasn't going to take all the little remarks and slights. People misunderstood me just like they misunderstood Albert. Albert Belle wasn't hearing no slave jokes around him, and if he did he was going to mess somebody up.

Once he got mad, he became a villain. Once they paint you as a villain, that's what you are. Same thing happened to me, and it came from racism, it came from bigotry. They were more comfortable around Stepin Fetchit players. They weren't used to a black man being proud and outspoken, weren't used to him speaking his mind when opinions differed.

Albert was hitting. And while he was hitting he was saying and doing what he wanted to do. You see, Albert was born in Louisiana and called a nigger every day of his life. His dad, his mama, his aunts and uncles—everybody in his family heard it every day, all the way back to slavery. So any time that Albert got upset, believe me his deepest, darkest thoughts were about growing up a child in Louisiana—just like mine are of Mississippi. And I'm sure he has stories worse than mine. But nobody ever asked. Nobody ever asked why Albert was upset, or why Milton Bradley is like he is, or why Carl Everett is like he is.

I know all those guys and I know how they grew up and where they came from. We got everything in common—and I can name 50 more black ballplayers who played in the major leagues that come up the same way, and all of them didn't play for a long period of time in the major leagues either. When they should have played 15 or 18 years, they only played eight or 10 years. Thirty years old and they're out of the damn game.

If you knew how to kiss tail and listen to the slave jokes, you played 15 years.

So many things I heard I didn't accept and I would lash out. But it couldn't kill my love for the game. I've had people ask me how I can love the game so much when it's been so bad to me. The answer's simple: I just never let my personal demons get in the way when I was on the field. *Playing* the game, I was fine.

I was only distracted off the field. That was where I had to put up with personalities that didn't respect that I came from a strong background of blackness and awareness of who I am. I don't kowtow. I've always been tough. I know that I came from badass African forefathers. And I'm also fourth-generation Indian, and I know my background there. I know I came from

98

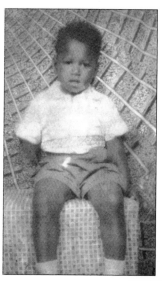

A picture of me at three years old, taken at the fair in Meridian, Mississippi, in 1962.

Summer of 1972: I was named the MVP of the little league all-star game in Hattiesburg, Mississippi.

After my freshman year at Jackson State, here I am with the Sandflat All-Stars in 1978. I'm in the top row, second from the right.

It wasn't long before I was pitching in the big leagues. My first year, 1982, and I'm staring down hitters in Yankee Stadium. (Courtesy Getty Images)

Karen and I attended Roger and Debra Clemens' wedding in Texas in 1984. We were married the next year in Meridian.

Celebrating a win over the Yankees in 1985 with (from left) No. 15 Marc Sullivan, Wade Boggs, and Dave Stapleton. (Courtesy Getty Images)

And then there was 1986 and the World Series. Here I am jumping out of Keith Hernandez's way after tagging him out at first base in Game 3. (Courtesy AP Images)

Spring training 1987: Sitting outside of the clubhouse with Karen, who is six months pregnant with our son.

John McNamara and me having a conversation in the dugout.
(Courtesy Getty Images)

Pitching through injuries in 1988. Here I am reeling back to throw in
a game against the Mariners in the Kingdome. (Courtesy AP Images)

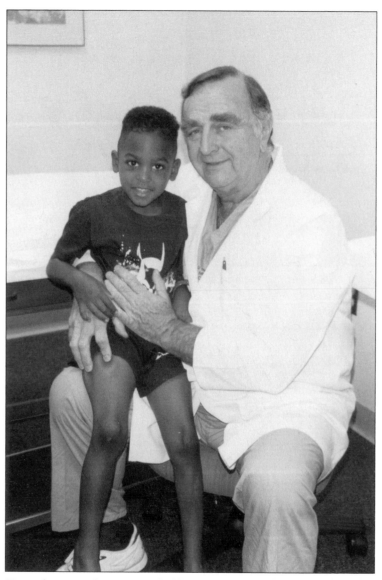

Team doctor Arthur Pappas holds my son, Dennis II, before I go in for surgery in 1989. Dr. Pappas was a good friend and a good man.

Pitching for the Montreal Expos in 1990. This was one of the happiest years of my career. (Courtesy Getty Images)

The most important thing in life: family. My father-in-law, Dr. Isadore Ramos; my daughter, Tala; my son, Dennis II; and my mother-in-law, Lorraine Ramos.

Still doing what I love. Bill Lee (who I call "Space") and me sharing a laugh before a game between the Brockton Rox and Oil Can Boyd's Traveling All-Stars in Brockton, Massachusetts. (Courtesy AP Images)

warriors. I know that I came from a Choctaw race that fought, that wasn't a passive tribe. They were Comanches and they fought and I know that type blood runs through me; that's why my spirit was different.

Knowing about my background is a big reason why I wasn't intimidated by where I was. I might have been fragile, because I was sensitive and I cared about people liking me, but I wasn't intimidated. I couldn't be intimidated, not with the way I grew up. I grew up in a place where you had to show your manhood every day. You had to fight for everything. You had to be initiated into every goddamn thing you did in life. Even in your own household you had to stand your ground, because your brothers were tough and you had to take what you wanted.

7: Mexico, Mississippi, and Fort Dix

"I'd want to beat up my wife and kids, go smoke some dope, get a gun, and want to kill every banker that I saw that day."

Mexico,
Mississippi,
and Fort Dix

After the tryout with the Indians I was just sitting at home in Winter Haven in 1993, hoping that somebody would give me a chance. I had been out of the game a year and a half, but I was only 33 years old. I was looking for an opportunity to get back on the field and I got this call from a man by the name of Carlos Paz to come play ball down in Mexico. I had gotten a call from Jorge Orta to come to Mexico in 1992, but I didn't go down. I was still hoping that somebody was going to give me a chance. But the previous year, nothing happened.

So I went to Mexico in '93 and played in Monterrey for Industriales. I went down there in early May. The season had started already and they needed a closer. I had never closed games before, but I told them, "Yeah, I'll do it."

I got off the plane and I thought I was going to at least get a day of being able to get ready and stretch myself out. But as soon as I got there I went straight to the pitcher's mound. I set a record down there as a closer. I pitched 11 consecutive days and saved 11 games. I blew my 12th save and gave up a grand slam in Mexico City.

I pitched real well down there, but it didn't matter. I got released all the same.

It happened because of the difference in the way the game is played down there. In Mexico—like in Japan—it's not an aggressive game. They don't play it like we do in the United States. We pitch inside and hit people and charge the mound. We fight over here. In Mexico, they don't charge the mound. In Japan, they don't charge the mound when they get hit, whether you're trying to or not. There's no retaliation.

I wasn't used to playing like that. One night, one of our pitchers—who was a pretty good ballplayer—was getting killed. We were playing in Laredo, Texas, and he gave up like five home runs that night. I mean, they were banging the ball. Nothing inside, they were just free swinging up there. At one point they even hit back-to-back-to-back home runs. We pulled him and it was more of the same. I was getting kind of pissed because nobody had gotten knocked down. We gave up like seven that night, and we got beat 18–3. It was like batting practice.

So here we were, the very next night, playing the same team, but this game's being played across the border in Laredo, Mexico, which is called Nuevo Laredo. We're winning this game. Now, I was doing two- and three-inning saves down there, so I was used to going into the game in the seventh or eighth inning. This kid had pitched a good game, but in the seventh he gives up back-to-back home runs—and it's to two guys who had hit back-to-back home runs the night before!

I hollered from the dugout, "Man, knock somebody down!" That was like nine home runs in two ballgames. We done gave up. I said, "Man, somebody has to get knocked down, they're free swinging!" The language barrier was there but there were a few guys on the bench who were bilingual.

So the manager came to me and asked me to go into the ballgame. I said "No," and he got mad. He went and got an interpreter, one of the coaches on the team, and he said, "I want you to go get loose in the bullpen."

I said, "No, I'm not pitching unless the very next pitch he throws up there knocks this guy down."

He said, "We don't play like that."

"I'm not going out there unless this guy shows some balls and knocks this guy down." I said. "Even if he hits him or walks him, I don't give a fuck! Tell him that's what I said."

So, the very next day, since I wouldn't go in the ballgame, he got in my face. We had a little shoving match and he got tough with me, like he was going to make me pitch. I just said to him, "You're not making me pitch." So the very next day they released me.

I came home, kept myself in shape, and went back to waiting.

In '94, I got another call from Carlos Paz asking me to come play in Mexico, but in a different city. I played this time in the Yucatan, in Leoni. I pitched really well that year. I was 2–0, but still I got released. They thought that I was going to ask for more money in my contract because I was pitching so well and I was an ex-major league ballplayer. They knew that I thought that there shouldn't be anybody down there making more than me. Hell, I'm a premier player and if anybody down there is making eight or nine grand a month, then I should be, too.

I ended up in Sioux City, Iowa, a month later, with Ed Nottle. As soon as I left Mexico I got a call asking if I would come to Sioux City. When I got there, Ed put me on the All-Star team to go on this little tour. I got a chance to pitch against the Silver Bullets—Phil and Joe Niekro were running around the country with a girls baseball team. So I got a chance to pitch against them.

We actually made history when Michele McAnany, whose dad used to play in the big leagues, got a hit off me leading off the game, on the first pitch. She got the first hit by a girl off a male professional baseball player.

In Sioux City I played with an old friend of mine. He picked me up as soon as I got there, came to the hotel and picked me up. He had two girls with him, two pretty young white girls. He took me out to this little bar in Sioux City and once we got there I was sitting with one of the women and he was on the dance floor dancing with the other.

I needed to go to the restroom, and in the process I walked past some guys at the door in leather jackets, like bikers. One of the guys said, "Hey, Nigger, we don't like your kind around here."

I just kept walking and said, "You talking to me?"

He said, "Yeah, Nigger, I'm talking to you."

So I went to the bathroom, and when I came back they just looked at me. I went and sat down with this girl, but I was getting a little touchy. I was like, "I don't know if this is a good place for me to be right now." It was a mixed club, more whites than blacks. Not a lot of blacks in Sioux City. So I'm sitting with the girl and two guys walked up to the table. One of them, a tall, slim guy, said, "Hey, Adrian." I'll never forget he called me Adrian.

I said, "Man, my name's not Adrian, you don't need to be messing with me. You already called me a nigger and I didn't do nothing to ya."

"Well, you ain't going to do nothing to me, Nigger."

I said, "All right," and the girl next to me was getting nervous. I said, "You go get my buddy, get him off the dance floor."

She left and this guy said, "You sold me some bad dope."

I said, "Look, man, I just off a plane. I'm a ballplayer. I'm not from here. My name is not Adrian, man, and you need to leave me alone."

Well, I was carrying a gun. I had this Louis Vuitton bag but I didn't bring the pistol into the club. I left it in my friend's rental car. So these guys went back to staring at me from their perch at the bar, and while this girl was looking for my buddy on the dance floor I walked through the crowd, went out the door, and told the guy at the door I'd be right back. I came back in with the pistol in the bag. I sat back down, and by that time my friend had come looking for me. He said, "What's going on?"

I said, "Hey, man, that dude's messing with me."

He said, "Don't worry about it, man."

"Look, man, he done came over here and called me a nigger a couple times and we need to get out of here."

"No, man, don't worry about it." So he goes back to the dance floor. I'm like, I'm done with this fool. Then the guy came back. He's a big guy, and I told him that he had to stop that nigger shit, I'm trying not to get violent. Then he tells me that he's going to take me out to a corn field, tie me up, and set me on fire!

That's when I took the pistol out of the bag and I beat him upside the head with it. When I hit him upside the head, somebody hollered that I had a gun. His head was bleeding and the crowd started running out the bar, and in the process they called the police.

So after I beat him upside the head, here come the paddy wagons and all the police, bouncers, and everything. The policeman asked me if I had a gun. I told him, yes, I had a gun. He asked where it was and I said, "It's in my bag."

He said, "Get it out."

"I ain't getting shit out. It's right there. It's in the bag. You get it."

He opened it up and pulled it out. He said, "Ain't been fired?"

"I only beat him upside the head with it."

"Sir, who are you?" I had all these gold chains on and it made him think I was a dope dealer.

I said, "Man, I'm an ex-major league player."

"You're Oil Can Boyd? I read in the paper that you were coming. Come on outside, Dennis." He didn't put any cuffs on me and he was nice to me. When we got outside he said, "Tell me about what just happened in there." The other guy, they weren't even taking him to the hospital, they put his ass in the paddy wagon. I got to talking to them and told them what the guy said to me, what he did. The officer said, "Is the gun registered?" I told him it was. Then he took the gun and put me in the car, but he didn't handcuff me or anything

I went to court a few days later. I got in the courtroom, sat down, and waited. Eventually they brought in the other guy. They brought him up to the stand first, and as it turns out I never even had to go sit up there. It lasted five minutes.

The lawyer asked him, "From what I understand the incident started because you thought he was somebody that sold you some bad drugs, is that correct?"

And the guy said, "I was just saying that to him. I got jealous because he was with two pretty white women and I don't like seeing niggers with white women." He said that, right on the stand: "I don't like seeing niggers with white women."

The judge dismissed it just as quick as you please. In fact, he asked me to his chambers so that I could sign some autographs for him.

So here it is all over the news: "Oil Can Boyd Pistol Whipped a Man." But no one spent the time to find out what really happened. Still, even with the fact that I was only protecting myself and I didn't get in trouble, I stopped carrying a gun after that. I was too close to killing somebody. Having it on me just brought me too close to doing something I didn't want to do.

• • •

In '95, George Kalafatis called about being a replacement player. I didn't even know about the replacement players. I wasn't keeping up with the strike. I wanted to be in the game and I was looking for somebody to call me, and I figured I'd probably go back to Mexico or somewhere. But then George called and said, "Dennis, there's 20 teams that want you to come and be a replacement player." We talked about it for a little bit, and then I decided that I'd go and play with the Chicago White Sox.

I could have made the White Sox team—I threw the ball that well—even Kenny Williams said so in a meeting. I hadn't pitched in like six or seven months, hadn't been on the mound, but I was working out before I got over there. So my arm was getting stronger. I'm always going to throw strikes and do the things I know how to do. I just didn't have the velocity on the ball.

I was messing around in the outfield one day, taking ground balls with Rob Dibble and Michael Jordan (this was when he was playing baseball with the Sox), when all of a sudden I was told to come inside. Then I was sat down in an office while some people with the White Sox said that drugs had been found in my hotel room.

I said, "You ain't found no motherfucking drugs in my room. What drugs you find in my room? Maybe some pot. Everybody knows I smoke pot. So what're you talking about? Why you got me up in here about some weed?"

Then they told me that it wasn't about weed. They'd found something stronger than that. They'd found syringes.

I said, "There's supposed to be syringes. I take blood thinners so I can throw this damn ball." I told them that they were prescribed for me. They had forgotten that I had gone through the thrombosis in Boston, that I had to take blood thinners to throw the baseball. Every time I get to throwing the ball hard I have to stick myself in the stomach with a needle.

So I got my whole medicine cabinet with me in the room—got these little things of Heparin. I stick the needle down there, I shoot myself up. In the morning, I get up and blaze, then I take my shot. I break the needle head off and throw it in the toilet. Sometimes they don't go down, though I hadn't really cared until that point.

Apparently the maid came in the room and smelled weed, and then she looked in the toilet and saw a syringe and she was like, "Oh, we got us an addict."

So while I was on the field the police came in and seized my weed and my medicine. They took it to a lab to find out what it was. While I'm on the field they're doing this, and I don't know it. I said, "I'm going to the hotel." And I left.

I went to the front desk at the hotel and said, "Who let the police in my room? That's my shit. You cannot open that damn door without me in here."

They got nervous as a hell. And then a White Sox person came over there, because I had told them that I take blood thinners and now they were worried.

I said, "Look, I just got through throwing. I could die right now, while I'm talking to you if I don't have my medicine."

So then I had to go to the police department, and they knew that they were in the wrong, as well, for going into my room. So what did they do? They tried to make themselves look better. I was sitting there, talking with the chief of police, and he said, "Well, we found weed in your room."

"That's no excuse," I said. I told them that they shouldn't have been in there in the first place. That's my weed. I want that weed. Shit, I bought it down the street—right over there. I'm going to go get some more, as soon as I leave here, I'm going to go get that weed. So either they could give me that weed or they could follow me down to where I'm going to get some more.

And then they gave me back my weed! They gave me my weed, drove me back to the hotel, and I went back to the ballpark. I got dressed, went back on the field, and nobody said a thing to me.

The next day I came to the ballpark and there was a pink slip waiting for me. They were releasing me. I said, "That's okay, fine."

They told me that I threw the ball really well, and said that they didn't want to release me. They asked me if I would go to rehab.

"No," I said. "I ain't going to rehab. I've been smoking weed every day since I was 12. I wouldn't even be here if I weren't high. I wouldn't go nowhere near a pitcher's mound. Now, if I was on some heroin or cocaine, I'd be telling y'all to put me in rehab. I'm telling you to leave me alone and let me go do what I been doing for the last 16 years. I've been pitching high on weed for 16 years. And you already knew that."

Two-thirds of the ballplayers I played ball with smoked pot. Not a third—two-thirds. But people don't want to hear that. People don't want someone around telling them truth. That's why they wanted me gone and forgotten. Marquis Grissom said it best when he told me, "They hate your goddamn name around baseball. When someone mentions your name, every coach everywhere gets upset."

• • •

When I first left Mississippi it was the Ku Klux Klan that held you down, but it's a lot more subtle now, a lot sneakier. When I came back, it was a whole different element of people that were involved. They were like the sons and grandsons of those Klansmen, but still they had a strong state of keeping people oppressed. The government and the banking industry and all those in power down there run things differently. I was just getting off of the ballfield and saying, "Okay, they won't let me play Major League Baseball no more, then let me see what I can do with my money pertaining to baseball."

I got into real estate when I first got back to Meridian. I was learning a lot in a short amount of time. But my real reason for going there was to put professional baseball in my hometown.

In '95, I'd been in Sioux City, Iowa, playing for Ed Nottle and the Sioux City Explorers. At the end of the season I saw that a new league, called the Big South, was being formed. As I was reading the schedule, it came to my mind that I might take a look into this. But I'd already agreed to play in Bangor, Maine, for the '96 season, so it kind of put me back a year.

So in '97 I went down to Meridian in the hopes of buying a minor league franchise and building a stadium right there in my hometown. There used to be a team there, but they'd folded up a few years earlier.

I was also building some spec homes down there, hoping to enhance my hometown. What you have to understand is that where I grew up is a poverty-stricken area, literally one step up from a third-world country. I wanted to improve my particular neighborhood where I'd grown up, too. The land I bought and developed was around the corner from my grandma. Down the street was my dad, and around the corner was a brother. I had several hundred relatives within an eight-block radius. It was my neighborhood, my borough, my town.

Why weren't these projects successful? Because the city wasn't behind us and others—friends and ex-major leaguers— were afraid to invest their money in a place like Meridian, Mississippi. That city has a background; it has a bad history.

I spoke about it in '90 when I signed to go play for the Montreal Expos. I was interviewed by a writer from the *Montreal Gazette*. I spoke about growing up there as a kid, and what it was like for our parents, and how the city was back then and now. A lot of people took offense to it in Meridian. They didn't like that I was telling the truth about the town and its ugliness.

They even took to saying that I would never have a road named after me. Normally in the South, in these small towns, if you're a famous guy like Jerry Rice or Walter Payton, then you get things named after you. I'm sure if you went to their hometowns you'd find roads and things named after them.

And that sentiment was still there when I got back. They didn't want to see me do well. They weren't proud of me when I left and they weren't proud of me when I came back. That's basically the way it was.

I was paying for the housing project out of pocket, and I started looking for a loan so I could start up the ballclub. Thirteen banks said no, absolutely no. I heard things about how the black people down there didn't have the money or the inclination to get behind this, and the whites in the city were not going to endorse a black man running and owning a professional baseball team. They were not going to be behind a black man owning anything down here. This is what a banker told me directly to my face.

I spent a little over a quarter of a million dollars developing property and building homes. I built some nice homes in a black neighborhood. I built them there purposely for that. It seemed like everyone who wanted to move in, though, was denied financing for one reason or another. I went to 20 black families in the city, and 13 of them wanted to buy the homes. I told them how to get their papers and such in order, how to go through the bank; but the banks turned them down. These were working, prominent people. Banks wouldn't let them own anything. They told them that their credit line was too messed up. That's why more than two-thirds of the blacks in the town that I grew up in rent homes. A very small percentage of black people own homes down there.

I wanted to lift my people up and give them something to be proud of. I wanted them to have something of their own, and not just a nightclub that we own downtown, or a little juke joint over in the neighborhood, a little store on the corner. Because that's already what the South consists of.

We know that this man who came over here—couple hundred years ago—he took these Indians and did what he did with them. He made himself a great world out of it. He used other people's blood and backbone to build and gave no restitution or reparation afterwards. And I don't want nothing. All I want as far as restitution is that they let me go into business and help my people. And I was denied that, flat-out denied it. That's my restitution. I'm a slave descendant and I wanted to help my people. I wanted to take this million dollars that I made and spend it on my people. But the bank took it all, just for that notion.

Part of the reason they said they denied our loan was that they didn't want me to use my own construction company— which was my family's—which had been in the business more than 35 years. These were qualified workers, but they denied us the project and denied us the money. Mind you, we were borrowing against our own money! We didn't come in there asking for money without any of our own. We went in there requesting a certain amount against our money. We were ready to put up a million dollars. We went to them asking what can we get for a million dollars for this many years.

There were other black contractors that wanted to do business in Mississippi, too, and who had been denied. They found out that I was denied, and so they wanted to bring a class action lawsuit against the banks. I spoke with 30 attorneys in the state of Mississippi and not one would take my case against the city of Meridian or the banks in that area.

I think they were scared. I think people got in touch with those attorneys and told them what'd happen to them if they represented us.

And this is the kind of stuff that I had to fight against, the kind of stuff that I had to live through. People talk about what I've been through on the field, but it can't compare to what I went through off the field. It's not even in the same realm.

Who are you once you come off the baseball field? It's a scary world. It's *real* scary. You think that people are proud of you, want to do business with you, or let you do business. You think that you've done something in this world, but really you ain't done shit.

I'd go home after spending $100,000 on developments and watching it go down the drain and just be madder than hell. I'd want to beat up my wife and kids, go smoke some dope, get a gun, and want to kill every banker that I saw that day. I wanted to kill everybody that I ran into, everyone that messed with me about my project and didn't pull for me. I went to bed dreaming and thinking, and sometimes not going to bed for three or four days from staying up doing dope. And then I'm going to the bank the next day, taking out another $50,000 because this property over here needs it.

The angrier I got, the higher I got, and then I'd get angrier because of that. I was this far from exploding. So I had to turn it all loose and in the process I got separated from my family. Karen went up north, because we weren't in a good atmosphere. I was living dangerous and something bad was bound to happen. So in a way, her leaving was the best thing that could have happened. Maybe I should have left, but I stayed four years, because I had almost $1 million down there in the ground. I didn't want to leave it, not unless somebody put me in the ground. That's what I was thinking.

What kept me from going over the edge? My kids, my family—yearning to be with my family. You have to want to live. If you want to live then you can straighten out that other stuff—material things, homes, and cars, all that stuff will come back. But you ain't getting a new life.

When my wife was away I met a girl named Renita. We hung out together for a little while, while I was trying to get myself back together. She helped me a lot. Then, out of nowhere she died from an aneurysm. She was only 37 years old and everybody in my hometown, all the blacks in my hometown, swore that I gave her some drugs. So they gave her an autopsy, and just like I'd been saying, she didn't have any drugs in her system. She didn't do drugs. She smoked some weed, but she didn't do nothing with cocaine or anything like that.

Everything was just everybody's business there. The most envy and the most hard times I ever had was with family at home. I'd ride around the corner and two-thirds of the guys that sold me crack were my cousins. These weren't strangers. One of my first cousins, 17 years old, sold me some crack. But that's going on in the whole city because everybody is related to everybody. That's the real incest. That's incest in life. Everybody thinks incest is fucking, but it ain't. True incest is when you got people that should be loving each other and instead they're killing each other.

• • •

A little after Renita died, I moved out of Meridian and I was staying in Tupelo, Mississippi. I met this lady and we hung out for a year or so. At the time I still had a lot of my major league belongings and personal stuff. We were staying together, so she had access to all that stuff.

I knew I had to get out of there or I'd die there. I left $1 million and went back to my wife, because I couldn't wait to get my life back together, and my life was my wife and kids.

I let taxes have all the land. I let it all go. Everything. I lost it in foreclosure. I'm still paying the government today for that land. I'm paying for every bulldozer I pushed, every house I tore down, everything I tried to build down there. But I let it all go, because when my wife and kids weren't there, none of it mean a thing to me anymore.

And I kept my wife. I've been married 27 years and that makes me more proud than anything I will ever have. I'm with my family, and that's what keeps me right. Some of the other guys, they lost their families, because they didn't have the type of wife that I do. They didn't have the type of person who understands that they love you, not what you do. They love you now, they loved you then, and they're going to love you in the end.

So that was that. I left and went back up to Providence, and I played ball that year for the Brockton team, but I left a lot of stuff there. She got upset that I'd gone back to my family and she threatened to burn up everything that I owned.

In the process of trying to work all this out I made some phone calls across state lines, which became a felony. She turned the recordings of the calls over to the feds. She took some advice from somebody at her job who she'd let hear one of the messages that I left where I threatened to beat her ass if she burned my stuff. She took it to the police and the police said, "This ain't nothing." So somebody told her to take it to the feds. In my opinion, the feds really made it into something because of who I was, not because of anything I did.

I wasn't doing anything but talking to this woman, but because I was talking to her long distance I got sent to jail. I was up north with my family and she would call me every other day. She called a few times to say that if I didn't come back she was going to burn up all my stuff. I said, "You ain't burning nothing." Then she'd call the next day and say the same stuff, so all these calls added up to five or six calls across state lines.

I was indicted on five charges of calling across state lines, making threatening phone calls. They said that I threatened to kill her, her son, and her grandkids, and burn up her house and everybody in it.

I had to go back down there to surrender. I flew back down there and surrendered to the FBI, by myself. They sat there and they asked me some questions. One of them asked me, "Do you have a drug problem?"

I said, "Not that I would *admit* to."

"Great answer," he said.

"Shit, you're going to have to catch me with something, doing something—you're going to see me in a straitjacket before I tell you I got any kind of problem."

They didn't even handcuff me. They took me over to the next county. We had to go over there and process everything. They snuck me out the back door. They didn't know if any media would be there or anything. They were pretty fair with me, but I didn't like going in courtrooms. I especially didn't like going in a courtroom with a goddamn rebel flag hanging behind the judge. They were talking about giving me some justice—that was scary—I thought I was in the movie *Mississippi Burning*. I swear in my mind I was in front George Wallace or Bull Connor or something.

That's the most intimidated I've ever been in my life. Then after a while, I wasn't intimidated any more. No, instead I got mad. You can tell me that you got the American flag flying with the Confederate flag, but all I can see is that rebel flag up there. And I know what the courts did to Emmett Till—they let murderers walk right out of the courtroom. I knew what a courtroom could do. I'd seen the same thing with Medgar Evers, same thing with James Chaney.

In the process I learned about the fears and the phobias that I had as a kid being brought up in the South. In the South, in that period of time, African Americans were very intimidated by police, by the justice system, by the whole thing. The things that I experienced as a kid growing up and heard about and saw from a distance, of how blacks were being treated, from the whole civil rights movement up until today, I just never trusted that I would get fair treatment.

Basically, everything that was addressed in the indictment was ultimatums; there were no direct threats. There were ultimatums. The words "if" and "then" are powerful words. "If you do something to me then I'll do something to you." It's an ultimatum. I knew that. I'm the one pretty much got myself out of trouble, by knowing that all I did was make ultimatums. Basically all they had was that I made some calls across state lines. But the calls themselves weren't much, so they put me on probation.

I personally felt that the whole thing should have been dropped because there were no charges brought against me. But it seems to me that the case became very personal for some. The judge said he wanted to take immediate action against me and say he wanted to oversee my probation.

After a while on probation they said I had to go to rehab or jail. I wasn't on anything when they made me go to rehab. But basically, what it was was that they didn't have any rehab places for me up here—they were all charging a whole bunch of money. I told the feds that they were sending me to rehab so they could pay for it. But they made me pay for my own rehab. They made me use my own money or they were going to put me in jail. It's a wonder they didn't make me pay for my meals while I was in there.

They couldn't find room for me up in Rhode Island, where it was going to cost like six or seven grand. I told them that I wasn't going to pay that kind of money out of my pocket. I wasn't going to put myself in the hole for them. So they found a rehab down in Mississippi and they charged me like $2,500 to go into rehab.

In the process at rehab, you have to go in the room and talk about it. "I'm an addict," and all this kind of stuff. You had to talk about your life with a whole group of people. They got little classes that you have to go to. There was this black girl in there who was on crack real bad and in the neighborhood where she grew up there were crack houses everywhere. She was telling her story about how bad it is, and then all the other kids get a chance to make comments.

So this one white kid said to her, "Why don't you just move?"

I didn't say nothing at first. The doctor saw me over there getting antsy because I didn't like the way this kid was talking to her. I didn't say nothing but I was getting upset. He could see me wiggling my leg and he said, "Dennis, you look like you want to say something." I asked him if he was sure about that, and he told me he was. So I start going off on this kid, letting him know that it don't work like that. You can't jump up and just move. She can't jump up and move! Moving takes money. She ain't going nowhere. She lived in a black neighborhood and it's filled with crack. That's where she born and raised. Where the fuck is she going to move? "You answer that goddamn question before you go saying that crazy shit that you saying." I said.

Then he said something else, and I got *really* mad and I was going to whoop his ass.

So my probation officer called me into a meeting later on that day. He said, "You're just a ticking time bomb ready to go off." I told him he was right. I am mad. I'm mad about the whole situation. I'm mad about the feds messing with me and putting me in this place. He said, "I'll tell you what, Dennis, we going to put you on probation *in here.*"

I said, "No, you ain't putting me on probation in here." Probation in there is not speaking for a day. You don't even open your mouth the whole day. I told him that the other guy was the one up in there saying offensive stuff and showing that he was a bigot.

So then they said that they were going to kick me out of the rehab, but I ended up staying. I finished rehab, but nothing changed. Next time a piss test showed that I'd smoked a joint that judge said I had to go to jail. He said he was sorry, but it was the law. So he gave me 120 days.

• • •

I wound up at Fort Dix Federal Penitentiary. There were killers and rapists and murderers, and I was there for making some phone calls and smoking a joint.

Once I got there, everybody knew me. It's the strangest thing, but the prisoners, they know who's coming to jail. All it takes is for one prisoner to get a call from their friends. "Look, Oil Can Boyd's on the way up there."

I turned myself in down in Mississippi. When I turned myself in they put me in jail for like 21 days, in a little holding cell. Then they took me to another jail in Mississippi and kept me like 31 days. This, as I found out, is how it is when you're in transit. They keep you until a bed opens up so you can go to jail. If they don't have a bed for you then you have to wait until somebody gets out.

So I went to this jail and that one. I went down to Oklahoma and stayed in a little jail for like 21 days. I moved around in that jail from cell to cell. In the process, a guard heard me talking to a guy. He said, "Hey, man, did I hear you say a little while ago your name's Oil Can Boyd?" From that point on, he snuck me some cigarettes and stuff. He was a big Texas Rangers fan and said he'd seen me pitch.

They were good to me, all the way through. Even the marshals on the plane. They flew me on that *Con Air* shit, where you got 500 criminals on the plane, chained up and cuffed together—and all that did was remind me of being a slave. When I dreamed that night I woke up having nightmares, because I felt I had been shanghaied. It was scary. And I was sad that I had got into trouble and I hadn't done nothing to nobody.

I was sad for a lot of reasons. I was sad because I felt like I was a slave all over again. I could see what it was like coming over here 350 years ago. Chained up. Shackled. And then I was ashamed—not of myself—I was ashamed for the people that put me in jail. They called themselves the police of the states. It made me realize that it was all about being black. All the time in jail I saw maybe three white guys, maybe 50 blacks. Then, when I got to Fort Dix, it was about 75 percent black to 25 percent white.

This plane takes you to a little private airport for holding—it's a jail airport. People don't know that they got airports just for criminals. They take you there and they put you on a bus. It was a two-hour bus ride with other inmates at 1:00 A.M.

I got to Fort Dix on June 2 and got out of there July 15. I already had a lot of the 120 days served while I was bouncing from jail to jail.

I didn't get any secret or overly special treatment at Fort Dix, but I was treated all right. The warden was an ex-professional baseball player. He played for the Mets in the minor leagues, so he loved me and loved baseball. I felt like the guards were looking out for me, but still, I was in with killers, cutthroats, every-goddamn-thing.

Where I was, there were 16 guys in there with me. The hallways filled up with men. We shared a couple showers, and you got time to watch a little TV. They'll play you a few movies, but they tell you when to go to bed.

I hadn't ever been in jail so I didn't know the attitudes. Believe it or not, I learned that over two-thirds of the guys that were in there had been there before. Nobody's a new prisoner. First timers are rare. So these guys knew the systems. Even in the little county jails that I went to, they knew what time you eat. They knew what you were going to eat. They knew everything. They knew the system and I was kind of getting in trouble because I didn't know the system. They tell you at a certain time you have to get up out of the bed and do roll call, no matter what. Few times I was still in the bed because I didn't know any better. The guards knew who I was, but they still had to show that they're tough on everybody. Still, they were like, "Hey, Boyd. Get Boyd up. Hey, Boyd. Next time you'll be on the floor." That type of stuff. Then they'd come to you later on in the day and say, "Hey, man, try to get with it."

One of the guys I met there had even graduated from my mother-in-law's daycare, the Beehive. He walked right up to me—muscle-bound guy—and he said, "Hey man, I know your father-in-law, I know your mother-in-law real well. I went to the Beehive." He said, "I remember you coming in there when I was five or six years old. If you need anything—or if anybody fucks with you...."

Then he told everybody, "Hey, this is Oil Can Boyd, he used to pitch for the Boston Red Sox. Nobody better fuck with him.

Nobody in this whole motherfucker." Him and another kid from North Providence, they looked out for me.

"You been to the commissary?" he asked.

I said, "Naw, I just got here."

He told me that I'd missed commissary that day. I told him that I had about $300 in my account, money my wife had wired in, and he said, "Don't you spend that. Don't worry about it." And you know what? I went home with that money.

He got a bag—one of them big-ass luggage bags that they gave us—and he went over to the ward where he lived. He started walking up and down the floor. He just went in folks' rooms and he said, "Hey, look, what you got in the cabinet? Give me them cookies, give me them chips, give me two of them drinks right there." He filled up my whole bag. He went through the jail just getting shit out of everybody's room and telling them it was for Oil Can.

I didn't shoot basketball or lift any weights in there. I played softball. We even had a team. We played twice a week. I would jog for recreation, a couple miles around the track, that type of thing. I'd hang out in the yard, maybe do a few pushups here and there. Basically, a few guys got to know you pretty well, and then everybody on the yard found out who you were.

I mean, I was in New Jersey. Everybody knew who I was. Soon as I said it, it was "Get out of here, man, that *is* Can." It was, "Yeah, I remember you, Dog. You a shit-talking motherfucker on the mound." You know, black guys—and mostly the whole ward was black—and some cool white kids from Boston, they all knew me. The white kids were in there for credit cards and fraud, the white collar crimes. The brothers were in for selling crack and shooting folks up. They were different criminals doing different things.

♦ ♦ ♦

After I got out I went back to my home, with Karen, where I belong. I don't go to Meridian anymore. Since my mom and dad have passed, I see really no reason to go back there.

That's how I feel about it. Basically the only thing that was bringing me back was when my mom was alive and my brothers and things. We would share my mom and dad, but now it's just us. But it's something that still disturbs me, and it probably always will.

Years ago, I was told by the administration of the Boston Red Sox, "You've risen up from poverty. You're out of that and don't look back." I remember I was very offended by that, but now I can see why they said it.

Don't look back.

I went to a seminar to hear about motivation and how to succeed in your life—the dos and don't and the wills and won'ts—and Colin Powell was there. Me and this other black guy were having a cigarette together. This guy was talking to me about being black and what Colin Powell stood for. I agreed that I used to have respect for the man, but I didn't anymore. I couldn't respect him after the way he went along with George W. Bush. This guy told me that I didn't understand, that it was about terrorism. You had to do certain things you don't like to defeat terrorism, because we can't have it in the world.

I told him that I lived through terrorism and nobody cared. I grew up black in Mississippi. I grew up in terror my whole life. And it wasn't an Iraqi calling me a nigger. It wasn't a Saudi selling me crack cocaine. It wasn't an Iranian who drove through my neighborhood shooting it up. It wasn't an Afghani who kept us in economic bondage.

So for me, being a black man from Mississippi, I can't see the world or the country like people pretend it is. I'm heartbroken. It goes all the way back to slavery—it's still about slavery. People make it seem like it's such a long time ago, but in actuality it ain't been that long. I got a grandma who's 105 years old right now, so it ain't so long ago.

I still try to go out right now, in life, and hold my head up high. I don't hold it up because of my accomplishments, because I don't feel like I accomplished anything. It was just a job and I was good at it. That's not being modest in any kind of way. I actually feel like I sort of failed, because I didn't get a chance to excel. I'm looked at as an underachiever, but I can't achieve if you don't let me play.

My whole life had revolved around baseball, and in a lot of ways it still does. I recently had a premonition that I was playing a ballgame at 52 years old, and I'm looking forward—if everything goes right—to lacing up my shoes at 72 years old, playing in senior baseball. That's how much I love the game. I know that's what's going to keep me living and functioning in the world. I have this dream that one day I'm sitting back in a rocking chair and watching some kid who I taught and fostered as he steps on the diamond for first time in the big leagues.

8: The Love's Still There

"He was the smartest

pitcher I ever met."

The Love's
Still There

I will always be a Red Sox!

To be drafted into the Red Sox organization is a special thing if you understand the history of the game. The Red Sox are a historic baseball organization, one of the first. And to be part of that is amazing. I wouldn't have the same feeling if I came up through the Seattle Mariners or the Toronto Blue Jays organization. I came up in an organization that had great history and tradition.

But I was also a black man being drafted by the Red Sox, and that had its own kind of history. I guess that would have been different, too, if I was drafted by the Mariners or the Blue Jays. I mean, this is a baseball team that's been around a long time, and was the last to sign an African American ballplayer.

That whole thing made it challenging. I even think it made me a true Red Sox, more so than I would even be as a white ballplayer. Knowing that an organization that didn't have a history of desiring African American players at one point—they waited 12 years after Jackie Robinson debuted to bring an African

American to the major leagues—wanted me and drafted me, that meant something. Some people still think of the Red Sox as a racist organization, but I don't think so. I think the modern-day Red Sox organization—front office on down—has tried to change that image. And they have changed it, all the way down to the camaraderie of the ballplayers, the atmosphere, even the fans.

Modern fans are more informed and more involved. Since the game is much more commercialized, it lets the fan get much closer to the ballplayer. The Internet is responsible for a lot of that. One search and you can find out what a player hit in college or the minors, where they're from, if they've ever been in trouble with the law, if they've ever held out for a contract, and on and on. It isn't like it was 30 years ago. It's not just the front of the jersey anymore.

It's just amazing how the Red Sox fans—and especially the ones from New England—know the game of baseball. They understand the managerial moves, a player should have caught a ball but didn't give it a good effort, pitcher made a bad pitch. The fan knows it up here—more so than a fan, say, in Nebraska. Baseball up here is like second nature.

I can sit around up here and talk to just about anybody. "So and so shouldn't have made this pitch last night." I mean, two 80-year-old women are talking about, "These guys are too comfortable up to the plate. They need to be pitching inside."

So I could feel the fans' pain when the 2011 season fell apart like it did. And it wasn't just that last night, when they lost to the Orioles and the Rays passed them by, it was the whole season. I could see the season unfolding like that, because the game is not won by a general manager paying a whole bunch of money and thinking that's just going to give you a winning season. The Yankees are an organization that is known for that, but a majority of their championships came when the Yankees had an advantage in the game, as far as being able to get all the talent that was out there. All the talent wasn't as equal back then.

It's about more than spending money. When they say you have the highest payroll, that's not going to get you a winning team. That's not assuring you that you have the best baseball players in this day and time. You can't tell me that Michael Young down in Texas is not as good of a player as Alex Rodriguez. I don't care if A-Rod hits 50 home runs or not—if I had a chance to put somebody in the batter's box in a clutch situation, I'm putting Michael Young up there. The game's not designed like that.

So you can't blame a Theo Epstein. It's the market that's driven up the prices and you can only get the ballplayers that're available at that time. Occasionally that'll lead to a bad decision, say on a Carl Crawford or a John Lackey, and that's going to be something that you have to live with. But I can tell you, it's not going to be a good seven years for Carl Crawford in Boston like they think it is. It's not going to be a good seven-year marriage at all, because people have high expectations and I don't think he'll ever have the season Jacoby Ellsbury had. And Jacoby Ellsbury's going to have to get paid, too.

The Red Sox have to understand: you put yourself in that situation. Also, you might have signed Dustin Pedroia for four years, but now you probably won't have the money and he's going to become a free agent a few years from now, and he's a better ballplayer. You're not going to be able to get him for $40 million like the last time. You're about to give a second baseman $100 million in another four years if you're going to keep him. So, you'd have come out better letting Pedroia play like we played, on one-year contracts until you become a free agent. Then if they want to walk, they walk.

I've never seen so many contracts being eaten as I have in the last 15 years. These players get these outrageous contracts, which I have no problem with, but then they don't perform. Either their game goes south or they can't stay healthy. Mo Vaughn was a bust in a contract. He didn't do a thing in California, and he didn't do a thing with the Mets. I know he got hurt with the Angels, but in my opinion an ankle doesn't usually keep you from playing ball for five years.

Albert Belle. Same thing. He went to Baltimore and he got a bad hip. Did these guys get hurt while they were there? Were these guys injured before they got there? You never know. But to me it just looks like you gave a guy a whole bunch of money that you didn't get nothing out of. Bo Jackson played with a bad hip, so it can be done. You can have a hip operation. Now, I don't know if that would've helped in Albert's situation, but he was going to end up a DH, anyway. He wasn't ever going to do anything other than hit doubles and home runs. He wasn't going from first to third on a single. So maybe if they'd given him a hip replacement they could have gotten their money out of them. I don't understand that—the guy walked home with $60 million and played a year and a half.

I saw the same thing with Pedro Martinez. Even though he came back, you knew he was hurt, and they still gave him what, $60 million? They gave him something like $60 million to go to New York, and he barely even pitched. Kevin Brown? Huge contract, but he didn't pitch that contract out.

It feels like almost none of them do anymore. I'm like, "Wait a minute, man, how can this be happening so much?" I've just never seen so many long contracts where the ballplayers aren't staying healthy and passing the test of actually signing a five-year deal and pitching out and winning, in five years, say 85 games. You almost never see it anymore. They'll sign a five-year deal but they won't win 15 games a year. Johan Santana's another one, and again because of injuries.

There aren't many of them right who will answer the bell. CC and Halladay, they're out there every fifth day. I think Cliff Lee is going to answer the bell. I think he will because he's so smart. He's not just a thrower, he's a good pitcher. He's left-handed and he has good command of that straight change-up—because velocity's going to leave; it always drops off. But if you master that straight change-up, like Cole Hamels and some others, then you can pitch for a long time. I can see that. But I can't see any right-hander that's losing velocity having continued success. I can't see Beckett going from 95 to 88 and still winning.

When pitchers get hurt or old they can't just turn into...well, me. Because that's what I did. I was pitching with an 85 mph fastball in Montreal and I had the best year of my life. You hear throwers talk and they're so afraid of that. I've heard them say, "I ain't got my good stuff tonight." That bothered me, because if you were a guy that only threw in the low 90s or high 80s, and you realized you didn't have your best stuff that day it didn't scare you, because you had learned how to pitch. So, if you lost a little bit—and that was me—then you had to know how to think, how to turn the senses up higher, and throw more change-ups. Pedro did that. You only see a few who can make that adjustment, especially right-handers.

Most right-handers that lose their fastball are done—you aren't going to see Roger Clemens come up with a knuckleball. It's pretty rare. Freddy Garcia has changed as he got older. He used to be a 94 to 96 mph fastball pitcher, but now he lives and dies on changing speeds and location, on his curveball and change-up.

But there's still nothing like the fastball. I remember when I saw Nolan Ryan and J.R. Richard throw a baseball when I was a kid growing up. I thought it was the craziest thing I'd ever seen. I couldn't believe that a man was throwing 98 mph. I ran to the TV. That was when they first came up with the radar gun. They were showing it on TV, Richard warming up for the All-Star Game at like 96 mph. I was amazed. "He's warming up at 96! Damn."

I didn't realize, seeing my brother Mike in high school, that he was throwing that fast, too. I heard he was "clocked at 97," but I was 11 years old, so I really didn't know what they were talking about. Until I saw him throw as I got older and I was like, "Goddamn, Michael could throw the ball 400 feet on a line." But nowadays, to see every kid throw a ball like that—like Daniel Bard in Boston or Craig Kimbrel in Atlanta—it's almost like they take it for granted. It's like it's just a different person throwing the same fastball. One guy's throwing 97 mph, they bring in another guy, and he's throwing 97. I remember watching a game recently and one team had a right-hander throwing 98; they took him out of the game and brought in a left-hander throwing 98.

Look at Kimbrel in Atlanta. I was watching a game in '11 where he was hitting 100 mph, and the announcers said that he'd pitched four days in a row. Now pitching four days in a row wasn't unusual to me. I could always do that, but I didn't have his velocity. I wasn't throwing 100. I think that hurt him. The adrenaline's flowing, you're overthrowing. So now you're out of the zone, now you're walking people. That's the part where being immature and young catches up to you.

Even pitchers like Papelbon, who have great stuff, if you stay in there and get enough at-bats, he will leave a ball out over the plate. If you foul off a few—like three or four pitches in a row—then you're going to get one. He can't stay in, in, in, out, out, out, out, all the time. I used to like it when hitters would tell me, when I'd see them the next day, "Can, you threw me six different pitches and they all were nasty and in nasty locations. I fouled them all off but I couldn't get to none of them. You threw me a great slider, you threw me a great curve, a great fastball, you ran a fastball in—but all of them are pitches I couldn't put in play." But so many young pitchers don't understand that.

Managers and pitching coaches don't know how to sit there and talk to the young kids. They don't. That's the best thing Bill Fischer and I used to do. That's what he used to love about me—that I would sit there and talk with him. That's when Walter Hriniak would tell everybody that ever met me, "He was the smartest pitcher I ever met." That's the first thing he would say to them, because, he'd say, "Can knows baseball and he knows pitching and he knows the game." I can't believe managers just don't sit there and talk to the kid. It isn't all about watching them in the bullpen or in the game, what they throw and all that—you have to talk to the kid. If you don't know what they're thinking then you don't know what they're trying to do, so how can you know if this was a mental or physical mistake, or if that was luck or skill. You can't know what you're seeing.

Like right now, if I was talking to Beckett—and he would listen to me—I'd make him a great pitcher overnight. Not a really good pitcher, a great pitcher. He'd go out there overnight and turn unhittable. And if he'd let me call pitches from the dugout, he'd throw a no-hitter. You just let me call pitches for you, and you throw the ball where I tell you to throw it. Believe me, he would see the difference. Two-thirds of my strikeouts in the major leagues came from looking, not swings. I struck out almost 800 batters, and I'd say half of them went down looking. That's what you call pitching.

I'd have 15 punchouts in a game and 11 of those struck out looking. How do you strike out 11 people looking? Nasty stuff ain't enough. Lots of people have nasty stuff. You got to set people up and then freeze them. You can freeze them when you got control. I used to do it all the time. I'd know that I was going to throw a straight change-up, and I'd know what I was going to follow it with, depending on what happened to that change-up. The guy's out front, does he pop it up, hook it foul, swing and miss? Either way, I already had a pitch to follow that pitch. It wasn't like the catcher had to call it.

That's why it bothers me when I hear that Varitek calls a good game and the pitchers depend on him. It ain't good when a pitcher feels that a certain catcher *has* to catch him. The best game I ever threw was to a catcher named Dave Sax. The best game I ever pitched in my life I pitched to him. Rich Gedman usually caught for me, but Geddy was hurt. Sax was nervous before the game, so he went to Geddy and asked his advice. He was nervous because I throw so many different pitches. He said that I did so many things out there and he didn't know what to do. Geddy basically told him, "Listen, all you have to do is what he tells you to do and you'll be just fine. Don't worry about signals, don't worry about location, don't worry about anything. He'll call all of it. All you have to do is catch it."

And Geddy was laughing when he came to me. He said, "Dennis, do what you do, because he's really worried about catching you tonight."

I threw a three-hitter. I think I threw 98 pitches that night, and I called all the pitches in the ballgame, every last one of them. Location and everything. And he would come back to the dugout and sit next to me and he would just turn—he had a big, pretty smile—he would just sit and smile and say, "That's amazing."

He would call a first-pitch fastball, and I'd shake away from it or I'd shake to it, maybe a different location. I want a fastball but I don't want it in, I want it away. Bam, throw my pitch. Next pitch, he might put down a curveball. I'd shake it off. I want a change-up—left-hander or right-hander, I want it away. A change-up should never be thrown in.

One night when Geddy was catching me I just froze up. Geddy called time and ran out to the mound and asked me why I didn't throw the ball once I got the pitch. I said, "Well, I wanted it in and up. I didn't want it in. I wanted it in and up and you didn't give me up." He hadn't thought to offer that, but he just said okay and trotted back behind the plate. Next pitch was high and tight, and it knocked the batter down. Then I threw my screwball and struck him out.

Young pitchers and catchers today don't understand how important it is to pitch inside. What happened to the 0–2 high-inside heat? High and tight is what backs someone off the plate, what intimidates. It doesn't intimidate the batter when you throw inside at their waist, not like it does at the shoulder. When the batter sees the ball anywhere up near his head or his face, automatically, that's fear.

That's one of the things that's changed in the game. It may seem like a small thing, but it's changed the whole way that the game is played. Not being able to pitch inside creates more opportunities for hits and widens the gaps in the outfield for a hitter. Mediocre hitters become above-average hitters and good hitters become great hitters without the knock-down pitch. The knock-down pitch is designed to stymie the hitter, because there are not so many aggressive swings. And you don't even need to throw it to every batter. You can throw one per inning, or one in the sixth and maybe knock one down in the ninth. It's part of pitching, more than a slider or a change-up or a forkball or a curveball, because none of those pitches mean anything if you don't have a knock-down pitch.

You can't expect a hitter not to put a charge into one of your pitches when everything you throw is consistently hittable. They're going to always hit it hard. The law of averages may say that the seven guys behind you will probably get to it, but as a pitcher you can't depend on that all the time. But you have to eliminate it more than that. If you don't protect one side of the plate, then the hitter becomes comfortable to hit the ball on either side of the plate. You have to say, "One side of the plate's mine the other side is yours. If I make a mistake and hang a breaking ball over the middle, you pound it. If I throw some shit stuff on the black and you hit it hard back at me or up the middle and it's this far off the plate, well I have to do something about that."

See, back in the day I could do something about that. I could throw the ball where the hitter couldn't reach it. That's where you get the strikeout slider where the guy's ass is sticking out. You don't see that no more. You don't see the batter intimidated at the plate reaching for a slider. No, instead they're busting down through it, fouling it hard off to right field. They're hitting it hard and the ball is way outside. And I'm like, "Come on, man, how can the kids get people out if you let them hit like that?"

There needs to be a meeting in the off-season and that rule needs to be changed immediately! You're not making the game better. You're not making the game safer—we've played it for over 100 years and haven't gave a damn.

It started at the lower levels, because they didn't want the little kids fighting; they didn't want the kids in high school and college charging the mound. But then they took that mentality all the way to the professional level, all the way to the major leagues. When really, you should be able to knock a kid down. In little league you're supposed to be able to knock a kid down. Even when I was 12 years old—and new to the mound—I knew that if I threw two curveballs and followed them with a ball up and in, then you wouldn't swing at the curveball I threw next. You wouldn't swing at it because you were afraid. And I knew that in little league!

So how can that be taken away from the game? That pisses me off, because now you're taking food off of my table. You're taking the advantage from me and putting it directly into the hitter's hands. The hitter's already got a helmet on—at one time in the game the hitter didn't even wear a helmet—and the helmets all include the protective ear flap. Now the hitter has armor on his elbow, on his foot, on his shin, everywhere. They don't have to fear sinkerballers any more. Bob Stanley used to break people's feet. When a big toe gets broken because the batter hit that sinking inside pitch straight down into his foot, that's part of the game. But now they've made it so comfortable that a hitter can go up to the plate and he doesn't even have to worry about getting hurt on accident, much less on purpose.

But now it's, "We have to limit that stuff because he has to be on the field." And what's driven that mentality? The money. They pay these guys so much—and these players are so brittle—that the owners have a heart attack every time one of them breaks a nail. It shouldn't be like that. It should still be, "No matter how much money I pay you, you still have to get the job done. It's still the game of baseball and we can't change how it's played just because we pay the players a lot more money." You can't do that. You can't protect your interests by changing the way the game of baseball is played.

• • •

After the Red Sox epic late-season collapse in '11, Nick Cafardo of the *Boston Globe* contacted me. Cafardo covered me with the Sox and still writes about sports in Boston. There had been rumors about drinking by Red Sox players in the clubhouse during the game, and Nick wanted my take on it. Here's the piece as it ran in the paper.

Hard for Him to Swallow[1]

Sox' drinking habits lead Oil Can to pop off

Who better to address the issue of beer drinking in the clubhouse than Dennis "Oil Can" Boyd?

"I was a drug addict and an alcoholic," Boyd said, "and I never once thought about drinking a beer during a game. Never even thought of it. If I'd have done that, I would have had Yaz or Jim Rice slap me in the head. It's amazing to me. I never even heard of that.

"This is a different breed of player now. They're so spoiled and feel so entitled. I did everything you can possibly imagine outside the ballpark, but once I got to the ballpark, my mind was completely on baseball.

"That was my living and I never took it for granted. I never wanted to jeopardize what being a major league ballplayer was and how lucky I was to be there.

"Having a beer during the game? Having a beer in the dugout? How do think you can do that? How does that even cross your mind? How is someone sipping on beer and another player is walking by and that player doesn't say anything?"

Asked if he ever consumed alcohol at a ballpark under any circumstances, Boyd said, "When I was in the minor leagues, we were playing in cold, cold weather and I once got the clubhouse

---

1   Nick Cafardo, **Sunday Baseball Notes**, *Boston Globe*, October 23, 2011

kid to go get me some Wild Turkey before a game so I could put it in my coffee to keep warm.

"But at the major league level? Never. You have to have some respect for the game. We always had beer in the clubhouse, but you never drank it until the game was over.

"Did I drink beer before I got to the ballpark? Sure did. Many times. I'd have lunch, have a couple, and come to the park in the afternoon.

"But while I had my uniform on, and I was supposed to be watching the baseball game? No way. I'm telling you, these guys are different. It was surprising to hear that stuff."

The whole thing made me think about a story from my days pitching at Jackson State. Me and a couple of my teammates got blasted before a game that I was pitching.

It was hot, like 95 degrees, and I was out there pitching, sweating profusely from the heat and the humidity. The alcohol came through my pores and my liquor-laden sweat got on the baseball. So I threw the ball up to the plate and the umpire called time and yelled out, "Somebody's been drinking. I smell liquor." My catcher was laughing hard. The umpire didn't know if it was the batter or the catcher, he just smelled liquor because it was on the baseball.

So he came out to the mound, but my coach beat him out there. The umpire asked me if I'd been drinking and I said I had. He didn't seem to want to kick me out, so he sort of hinted to the coach that maybe he should take me out. But at the time I had struck out like 12 batters, so my coach wanted me to keep pitching. Eventually the umpire gave up and went back behind the plate and I stayed out there and won the game.

9: Those I've Met
Along the Way

"Major League Baseball

broke up my family."

Those I've Met
Along the Way

Al Nipper helped me out in my career quite a bit. He's a good friend. He understood me when I first met him. He could pitch, he was smart, and he knew about the game. He helped me come up with the screwball, and he was kind to me all the way through my career. He told me that I went from a thrower to a pitcher overnight. It was thanks to him that it took place. I owe him everything for that. And what I've kept from that is a friendship and a love that I'll have forever, bro, if you're reading this.

I ain't got anything valuable enough to give him for helping me become the pitcher that I was. I appreciate him for looking out for me when I was a young kid down in Sarasota and Winter Haven, Florida, in instructional ball, not to mention in Bristol, Connecticut, and Pawtucket, Rhode Island, and throughout my whole career in the major leagues. Nip was a real good friend and I mean that.

Rich Gedman was great, too. There was no one like him. We didn't start out on the right track. In 1982, when I first got to the Sox, Bob Stanley and I had some problems when

145

I felt he was teasing me down in the bullpen. I felt that he was playing head games with me and it pissed me off. And still, today, I'm pissed off. Inside, I burn when I see Stanley, even though I'm shaking his hand. I still burn. I always felt that he changed the way my career went, because I think he was purposely making me mad that day. And then when I got mad, I feel like, in the eyes of the owners I was just an undisciplined nigger. And he didn't stop. Stanley was always trying to get me worked up.

But at the same time that I met Bob Stanley I also met Rich Gedman. While Stanley was teasing me in the bullpen I kind of crossed Rich up on a pitch. I threw a two-seam fastball when I was supposed to throw a four-seamer and I didn't tell him. I remember him yelling at me. Now, I was just a young kid. I was the same age he was but he'd had more time in the big leagues, so he wasn't naive to what was happening. He yelled at me, and I remember thinking that I was the only black kid there. I was thinking, I ain't just a ballplayer, I'm a black ballplayer. I ain't Stepin Fetchit, I ain't taking nothing from nobody. You can't scream at me like that. I'm from Mississippi, motherfucker, and I can't have that.

So I got bent out of shape. But through the years we grew to love each other. And he was never the kind of guy who said something to me wrong; it was always purely baseball. He did correct me sometimes for doing something, but he always did it the right way. I always say to everybody that I know, "It ain't what you say, it's how you say it." And I love Rich Gedman. He was the best catcher that I've ever pitched to. As far as physical, mental, emotional, everything. He was right there with me and he's still right here with me today.

The fact that we got off on the wrong foot and ended up so close, that shows the character in that man. He gave me the opportunity to be his friend and took the time to get to know me. He did that. And that's why we're still good friends today.

Same thing applies to Marty Barrett.

We didn't get off on the right foot, but I ended up loving B. And B ended up respecting me as a baseball player and a man. But when we first met he thought I was a thief. Somebody passed it down the line that I was stealing stuff from other players. You know, niggers steal shit.

That was when I was playing minor league ball in Elmira. Some guys tried to set me up by putting stuff in my locker and telling the manager that I was stealing. And then I had to threaten some guys and tell them that whatever is in my locker is mine. And if anybody tried to mess with it, they were going to get their ass whooped. And I meant it.

Those problems in Elmira lingered into spring training in '81. The first thing I heard about Marty Barrett was that he said I was a thief. But he got to know me and he realized those things weren't true. We ended up being real good friends. That's pretty much the way it was. We had a misunderstanding, but we grew to love each other.

Best teammate I ever had was Eddie Jurak. He understood me and I hung out with Eddie quite a bit. Eddie and I had some nice times. We chased and ran some streets, and did some things that ballplayers do. Only difference was, I was married and he wasn't. I guess that makes it kind of messed up, but hey, it is what it is. But Eddie was a guy who understood me. He was just a real good friend.

Eddie just took to me right away. Eddie was laid back, a real cool kid. I could tell that he had no problem with color. He was open with me; we were just close.

I was all right with Steve Lyons, too. It was just that we were in Boston, and what they used to say, "Twenty-five cabs for twenty-five players," was pretty much true.

I had lunch with Eddie a couple times. I had lunch with Al Nipper maybe one time, but besides that I never went to lunch with any other Red Sox. No ballplayer ever invited me to go eat or invited me to do anything. You had like one or two cliques—Steve Crawford, Bob Stanley, Mark Clear, they did everything together—but besides that it was pretty much every man for himself. We were just so distant from each other.

I talked to Reid Nichols every now and then but Reid was a real good dude. Reid was one of them religious-type cats—that's what he was known for. He didn't go out and drink. He didn't go out and carouse. He and Hurst both, they would move away from you in the outfield if you was talking about what you did last night, how you got laid last night.

There were a few—I didn't see Marty Barrett drink or do anything—who weren't out gallivanting. They weren't clubby guys. In order for you to be like that, you would pretty much have to hang with peers who ran all the time. And Marty, for instance, just wasn't like that.

I've never seen so many guys who didn't joke together, didn't bullshit together. I think that was just the type of ballplayer they drafted. Even the black ballplayers were conservative. I gave Ellis Burks the opportunity to open up, be himself, but that wasn't his way.

Johnny Pesky really loved Ellis. He really pulled for Ellis. When you got a Johnny Pesky pulling for you that's something. Believe it or not, that's what black guys needed—they had to have somebody like that who pulled for you or you didn't get anywhere. There were a lot of ballplayers who didn't have that and didn't make it. Lee Graham was an outstanding ballplayer and he got one week in the big leagues. Barely played. He never even got a chance to play and he possibly could have been a Gold Glove centerfielder.

Manager Joe Morgan said that Graham didn't belong in Triple A in '81. He was 21 at the time and Joe said he didn't belong in Triple A, that he wasn't ready for it yet. Shit, Lee's a good ballplayer, but they always had a reason for saying that. There was always somebody else that *they* liked, that they wanted there. Let me tell you, Ellis Burks was not a better baseball player than Lee Graham. Ellis Burks wasn't a better ballplayer than Chico Walker. I played with them both, but Ellis was the chosen one. He was a good dude and he had great skills, but Lee Graham was Superman on a baseball field.

One of my favorite teammates of all time was Dennis Eckersley. Eck didn't have a prejudiced bone in his body. Me and Dennis used to tease each other all the time when we were together in Boston. I used to call him a redneck, and he'd call me a blackneck. He'd tell me, "I'm Portuguese, that ain't a redneck."

I said, "C'mon, man, you white. And if your ass had grown up down in Alabama you know damn well you'd have had a problem with Negroes." And he'd just laugh. But he saw I was a good person, and we were always good.

• • •

People blame Bill Buckner, who was a great player and had great character and loved the game of baseball, for what happened in the '86 World Series. And nobody could play it as well as he did. I saw him play when I was a young kid, and I admired him when he was with the Dodgers. I liked the way he played baseball. See, we got National League baseball when I was 13 or 14 years old. That's when I got a chance to see him, and I liked what I saw. And then, 10 or 12 years later I'm playing in the World Series with him.

He admired me and he showed me some things about how to carry myself as a pro. I'm pretty sure he knew I was getting high, and while he didn't condone it, he told me that there were certain things you didn't do. He was that type of guy. He probably didn't approve of how I was living, but he wasn't messing with me either.

And that was true of Dwight Evans, too. Dewey was the same way. He was a big brother figure to me. The years that I was there, Dewey was great. But he was temperamental, too. Dewey would jump on you. There were times he straightened me out, times that we had a few words here and there and everything. But he respected me as a man.

I was never intimidated by where I was, so that's why I was like I was. Just because someone had 10 years in the major leagues, I wasn't going to let that intimidate me. I was going to respect the hell out of Carl Yastrzemski and Dwight Evans, and I expected the same. That's why I love them today, because they never disrespected me. They never showed me one iota of bigotry.

Dewey would stand up for me when I got mad. He'd met my brother Mike years before and the two of them really hit it off. So ever since I was young he'd looked out for me. He promised my brother that nobody would ever mess with me while he was in a Red Sox uniform. He told Mike that if anyone charged my mound he'd take care of them.

My locker was right next to Dwight Evans—24 and 23—my stuff was right with his everywhere I went. Sometimes I think he requested it, because he would be the one who would check on me. He'd be the one to tell me to go get the weed off my fingers, so they wouldn't see it. He'd tell me to go put the Clorox on my finger. He would tell me—just like I was his son—and I would run and do what he said. I wouldn't question him, wouldn't say a thing. I had big love for him and Bill Buckner, and Jimmy Rice, too.

Dewey was a good man. And he was an even better man with me in my latter days. Talking to me and letting me know that if I needed him in any kind of way, he would always be there in my life. And that was real special for a teammate. And that tells me about what kind of man I was, too, for somebody to feel that way about me. When misery was filling my life, he really made me feel like I was a good man and I know that he loved me.

It was similar with Jim Rice, but Jimmy was different. Jimmy was caught in between *where* to be and *what* to be in his life. I want to say that he wasn't a token brother, because he could play. He's in the Hall of Fame for a reason. But at the same time, we had differences.

He looked out for me as much as he could. Behind closed doors, he was really cool with me. But I always felt like he made a point of showing people that he kept his distance from me. Because, I guess, he wouldn't be in the Hall of Fame today if he didn't. Hell, I've seen people get kicked out of baseball because they respected me. So he had his differences with me and I had my differences with him, but overall, he was an all right brother.

I can't really talk about his stats or anything like that. You know, he's in the Hall of Fame. Regardless of how he got in there, I guess he got in there. What I feel doesn't matter. Somebody else thought more than me, but it was a real good thing that he got there.

But Jimmy had to have a secret life with me. He couldn't have an open life with me. Once he first met me and saw what kind of person I was, he loved me, but he couldn't show it. I think that's because Jimmy had been molded to be a certain way.

Now Clemens, he was something special. I loved Roger from the first day I met him. We're still cool today. I played a long, long time with him. He understood me. That's why he invited me to his wedding. I'm proud of him and his family. Regardless of whatever he did or didn't do, I love him to the bone. He can't do no wrong by me. And that's the bottom line.

I never really ran around with him too much. He stayed to himself. He didn't hang in any of the cliques or anything. And it wasn't that people didn't want to hang with him—shit, he's Roger Clemens! He was a good teammate on the field and he was a good teammate off the field. People stayed to themselves on that team. I did. Everybody did. So it wasn't unusual.

He was a good kid, and man could he could pitch! He's the true meaning of what power pitching is. *Power pitching.* Not power throwing. Power pitching. He could throw that ball wherever he wanted at 200 mph. That's why he won seven Cy Youngs. You can't take nothing away from that.

Ain't no steroids or anything like it going to make him do that. Nothing enhanced that. That's pitching. And a lot of that he learned from me. And if you call him and ask him he'll tell you that himself. Mentality. Attitude.

He was already a bulldog when he arrived, and when he saw that I could be a little bulldog, too, but without all that heat, he said, *If I can out-pitch this guy, I'm going to the Hall of Fame.* And he did it, and that's where he should be.

Tom Seaver was also real good with me for the few days that I played with him. He respected my pitching ability, which was more important to me than anything. I was in awe when I would sit down beside him and just talk to him. It's the same thing that I could say about sitting down and talking to Jim Palmer. Riding in the cab with him and Bob Uecker to the World Series, I was amazed at these great baseball minds. They were good men and good baseball people. Jim Palmer was a great pitcher, and Tom Seaver was, too.

• • •

Nolan Ryan was top of the line when I played with him in Texas. His wife took my wife in, which was very special, because my wife didn't feel like she was a part of things down there. But Nolan's wife and Bobby Witt's wife helped her out. Steve Buechele made me feel like a champ down there.

Nolan told me one of the funniest jokes in the world when I was there. He said we had all kind of "Cans" on the team. We had Domini-cans, Ameri-cans, Mexi-cans, Puerto Ri-cans, and we had *Oil* Can.

I enjoyed being down there and watching him play. Knowing that he was over 40 years old, that's how long I wanted to pitch. Hell, I wanted to pitch longer. I had the makeup to do that. But the game didn't see fit to let me.

Also, as a ballplayer, I wanted Reggie Jackson's respect.

I really didn't give a shit as a person, because I knew that he came from the era when black ballplayers thought that they were the shit once they got to the major leagues and everybody else in poverty didn't mean a thing. That's the way Reggie Jackson's attitude was to me.

Everybody else might say some other stuff about him, but I just wanted to prove myself to him on the field. Because he said about me, "Who's Oil Can? He's just a rookie." So I had to show this guy that he couldn't hit me. And I showed him that. The bottom line is that I won his respect.

I have really complicated feelings for Don Baylor. We called him Groove, and he was a big black Mandingo-kind of guy, but he had this white wife. That messed me up. It really did. I didn't know how to talk to him. I mean, he was a Southern black man, but he didn't show me that mentality.

That's what I loved so much about Wes Gardner. He was from my home and he understood me and loved me. That's what I loved about Mike Smithson and Tom Bolton, who were from Tennessee. I loved those kids who I played with from the South. And then there was Groove, who was a black man from the South, but who married a white woman and didn't seem to feel like the rest of us did.

I can't say that wasn't something that kept me at a distance from him. I couldn't really talk to him how I wanted to. When he did really try to open up to me was when he first came to the ballclub and we were leaving spring training for opening day. We were leaving to go to Detroit. We were riding on the bus together to the airport and he was asking me personal questions. He seemed to be very concerned and I kind of got warm to him.

I thought he would be like a big brother to me. He asked me how they'd been treating me, and he said that he'd heard some guys were messing with me and how no one was going to mess with me with him around. It made me feel good, I guess, like someone might be watching out for me.

But I guess my behavior was something that he didn't approve of, because then he started to distance himself from me. It started out all right, and he even came to me during the season when I was having problems with the whole drug thing around the All-Star break. There'd been a story in the paper around that time that talked about me going out and buying coke. It didn't call me out by name, but everyone knew who they were talking about. It said something like, "A tall, slim black man goes down to the park, driving a 500 Mercedes. Everyone knows who he is." I heard tell a reporter got the story from his brother, who was a cop.

Anyway, Don Baylor came to me and told me that he didn't want to hear about me over there anymore. He said, "Now get out there on the mound and throw that ball like I know you can." And when I would pitch really well, he would come to me and say, "That's the Oil Can that I know."

Don Baylor and Bill Buckner, Dewey, Rich Gedman, and Marty, those five guys rallied me to stay healthy and pitch us to the World Series. Those five guys. Every day, whether I was getting the ball or not, they were there. Just in the clubhouse, you know, Rich Gedman would walk by and rub my head or something and Marty would walk by and tap me on the back of the head. They all let me know that they cared without saying a word.

• • •

I really don't like to linger on Wade Boggs too much.

I always felt that he was a bigot, a modern-day Ty Cobb–type. I used to joke that if the ball was black he would've had 8,000 hits. In my opinion, he didn't like anything black. I don't think he even liked nighttime. He probably wouldn't even wear black shoes.

That's the way he was. A really good ballplayer? Yeah. A Hall of Famer? Yeah. But believe me, I didn't put him in the Hall of Fame. White people put him in the Hall of Fame. I don't think any black person would've voted for that motherfucker if they knew him like I did.

When my son was born I asked Wade if he would be the godfather. Now, I know that sounds crazy, but the thing is, I really liked and respected him those first few years. Especially as a ballplayer—as a hitter—I respected him. He was very unique, and *most times* he was an all-right guy.

155

Anyway, he didn't say anything about the godfather thing—yes *or* no. But during that time I felt like I was getting to know him better, and then he got in trouble with Margo Adams and that whole thing happened. We were all reading stories about ourselves in the papers every day, supposedly stuff that Wade had supposedly told Margo. That was when I was like, "I don't know what I was thinking about asking this guy to be the godfather of my child." I didn't want this guy to be associated with my family at all.

It's weird. I was feeling good about him and what an ideal person he would be to be the godfather of my child, basically admiring him, and it all changed. And it's not like he's all bad; he could be a genuine person. But it was almost like there were two Wades, but unfortunately the one side of him took away the good side. And it's a shame, because I loved his family—his wife and daughter—to death.

It all came to a head when we got into a fight in Cleveland. I was sitting behind Wade on the bus and we were getting ready to pull up to the hotel. Just in that small, 20-minute span, things kind of got out of hand. We'd gotten off of the plane from Baltimore, and a lot of drinking had been done on that flight. A lot of us had consumed a lot of beers and shots.

We had a bus that had the back door and the front door, I guess it was a city bus. Anyway, Wade started messing with Jeff Sellers, who was sitting with Ellis Burks listening to some Keith Sweat on their headphones (Ellis had a system that allowed you to plug two sets of headphones in). Sellers always hung with the black guys—he was a cool kid from Compton, California, who grew up with black kids. Anyway, Jeff was rocking and Wade called him a "white nigger."

I was sitting right behind Wade when he said it and I threw a punch at the back of his head. Now, everyone was already on edge about all of the Margo Adams stuff in the press. I was already madder than hell at him about all of that, so when I heard him say what he said to Sellers my blood got to boiling.

So then Rick Cerone tried to defend Wade and Dewey got mad with Rick Cerone and Wade. We pulled up at the hotel just then and Wade jumped out of the bus. I screamed, "What you say, motherfucker?" People were holding me back and others were ushering Wade through the lobby and up to his room.

I remember Rac Slider trying to hold me when I came off the bus. A bunch of coaches and stuff got in front of me and they wouldn't even let me in the hotel. I was trying to get in the hotel and they wouldn't let me in until Wade got up to his room.

Dewey and me were pissed off. Rick Cerone wasn't a bad dude, he was just trying to keep the peace. But Rick was trying to slow up Dewey, and Dewey took Rick Cerone down—hard.

When I got up to my room my wife was already there. The phone rang about 10 minutes later. It was Wade and my wife answered the phone. Karen said, "Dennis, it's Wade."

I said, "I don't want to talk to that motherfucker."

So I didn't talk to him. He talked to my wife, told her to tell me that he apologized, didn't mean to do this, didn't mean to do that.

So the next day, we get up and get ready to go to the ballpark, but they'd already called the Red Sox, the administration, Haywood Sullivan, all of them. They wouldn't even let me in the ballpark.

They told me to go back to the hotel and calm down, so I went back to the hotel with my wife and we watched television and hung out. We watched the game on TV because they wouldn't let me come to the ballpark. I was madder than hell, with Wade, with the Red Sox, with everyone.

I came to the ballpark the next day and I was all right. I did my work, did my running and my throwing. I watched the game and it was sort of like it never happened. Except it did happen, and I never forgot.

• • •

It astounded me when I met Johnny Pesky. He knew the dap handshake, the whole soul brother handshake, tapping on your hand and all that. He shook my hands—that whole thing—and he tapped on the back of my knuckles, and I knew then that he'd hung out over in Roxbury or something. I knew right away. I don't know where he's from, but that man's hung out with some brothers. He and Babe Ruth must have run around together or something.

JP was cool. He was suave, man. He was what you call dapper. I don't know if he was a ladies man, but I guarantee the ladies liked him. You could see in his young pictures that he was a very handsome man. He was real suave and laid back, and he wore these top hat–like things, like a type of Stetson, and when he would shake my hand he'd give me this real soft soul brother shake.

I could tell that he was with the times and he knew what was going on. When I'd come in he'd say, "Hey, Can, my man, what's happening'?" I would talk to him and I saw how laid back he was and I could imagine playing baseball with Johnny Pesky back in the day. Through the years I grew to really adore him. He just always showed me big love and respect when I showed up at the ballfield. And still today, even in his older years, he's still the same way.

When I got called up, I was with him quite a bit because he hit fungoes in the infield. We were getting ready to play the Detroit Tigers and I was standing by him. This older black man was sitting over in the Detroit dugout and he hollered, "Hey, JP."

"Yeah, Gater, what's going on, man?"

"Who's that batboy right there wearing No. 23? I've never seen a batboy with a number."

JP turned to him and said, "This ain't no batboy. This is one of our pitchers."

"Get out of here, that look like somebody's baby boy right there."

Johnny said, "Go on over there and talk to Gater."

"Who is it?"

He said, "Gates Brown—go on over there and talk to him."

So I went on over there and started talking to him, and before long we'd got to know each other. For some reason, I took to Gates like he was a granddaddy figure. Gates was cool. He was a real good ballplayer for the Tigers, and it just so happened that he played with Willie Horton, who is a distant cousin of mine. Willie Horton's oldest brother married my mom's first cousin.

Horton, one of the great Tiger sluggers of all time, is like family. I have a lot of family in Detroit, through my dad's side. One of my dad's younger brothers, Jake, quarterbacked in high school and moved to Detroit and now he's in Michigan's Hall of Fame. And there's a connection with him and the NBA. Chris Webber and Jalen Rose both grew up in Detroit and my uncle was their coach and their mentor growing up.

Now, a bunch of these guys moved to Detroit back in the early '60s. Two of my uncles, Mike (who they called K.T.) and Jake; my mom's two first cousins, Jake and John Young; and Barry Larkin's dad, Robert Larkin, took a caravan of station wagons up north to pursue professional baseball careers. Barry Larkin's dad ended up in Cincinnati, Ohio. He raised Barry and the whole family there. Barry's dad and my dad are first cousins, so Barry and I are third cousins.

Jake and John Young, my daddy said, probably were the best shortstop/second baseman that didn't play in the major leagues. The whole semi-pro baseball thing and sandlot thing back in the South was all family. Two-thirds of the players on the field were related to me as a kid growing up.

When I came to the major leagues in '82, Barry Larkin's dad called home to Meridian. He called my daddy—who he called Skeeter—and said, "Skeeter, there's a Boyd pitching for the Boston Red Sox that looks *just like you.*"

"You know who's baby that is?" Well, he knew already. The Larkins moved when I was like two or three years old so he had never seen me. He had seen my older brothers and sisters but they had never seen me. "That's my baby," my daddy said.

So we did the same thing. My dad called him when Barry made it to the major leagues. "Who is this Larkin kid playing at shortstop for the Cincinnati Reds?" My daddy already knew, of course, because Barry looked just like his dad.

So Robert said, "That's my baby there, too."

I was playing ball in the Red Sox organization in Double A in '82 in Bristol, Connecticut. And one of my college teammates, Curt Ford, gave me a call. Curt played with another third cousin of mine. See, Jake and John Young both had kids, too, and each brother named their son after the other brother. Curt was in the Florida State League with the St. Petersburg Cardinals and on his team was a black pitcher named John Young.

Curt and John got to talking.

"Hey, where you from?" John said.

"I'm from Mississippi."

"Mississippi? No shit? I got family there. Where from in Mississippi?"

Curt said, "I'm from Jackson."

160

"Man, I had a cousin, played at Jackson. He's playing for the Red Sox organization."

Curt said he looked at him. He started looking at him hard. He said, "Dennis?"

That was when Curt called me on the phone and said, "Hey, look man, there's a dude on my team that looks just like you. He walks like you, talks like you, acts like you ... everything. He's small like you, too, and his head's like yours. He says he's your cousin. His name's John Young."

John had asked Curt to get in touch with me, so then me and John got to speaking. We were cousins but we'd never seen each other. I finally got a picture of him a bit later, and I'll be damned if it wasn't like looking at a clone of myself.

He was a left-handed pitcher for the Cardinals organization. He went to Triple A and I saw him in spring training in '84 and '85 at the big-league camp. This kid could bring the rock, straight hammer, like mine, and a slider. Skinny, tall, long, and blowing cheese. And he had played with my teammate, and that shows you how small the world is, right? That we all got something in common and we all come from family trees and we are all descendants of Negro League ballplayers—and then I came to find out that all the years I played with Curtis Ford I didn't know that his mom's brother played in the major leagues.

That makes sense. Curt's a major leaguer, and that has to come from somewhere. Well, have you ever heard of Marshall Bridges? He's a black ballplayer who played in the '60s, a lefthander. He was Curtis Ford's uncle. That means that Marshall Bridges grew up playing semi-pro ball against my uncles and against Barry Larkin's dad.

So, it's a small, small world.

My college baseball coach had played against my uncle, and that's a big reason why I went to Jackson State. My college coach faced Uncle K.T. growing up, when they were both about 17. When I was pitching in high school, Jackson State sent a scout to come watch me. He was a bird dog for the Cardinals named Fred.

So he came to see me and he went back and told Coach, "That Boyd kid, he's got some good stuff, but he's really small. He probably only weighs about 130 pounds."

Coach said, "You think he's worth looking at?"

"He's got good stuff," Fred said. "I don't know if he's scholarship material or not, but you know who is uncle is, right?"

"Who?"

"K.T. Boyd."

Coach said, "Go sign him right now," and that's how I got to Jackson State.

My uncle weighed 133 pounds and threw 100 mph. My coach had faced him and he said, "Dennis, I ain't never seen nothing like it before in my life, and when I saw you I saw him all over again. I saw K.T. Boyd." There's a road named after him back in Meridian. (And check this out, because this is some real slave, negro shit. My dad says his brother don't have a real name. He gave himself the name "Mike." His real name was just those initials, K.T., and they don't stand for anything. They never even gave him a real name.)

• • •

Bill Lee is a very sweet and kind man. He loves baseball. Nobody loves baseball as much as he and I do, and it's for the same reason: it's the greatest game in the world. I always admired his game, but now that I've gotten to know him I admire him more for the person that he is.

Bill Lee is a throwback. Not just a throwback as far as the game; he's a throwback in life, too. He's a well-rounded person.

He can relate to people of all ages, all sizes, all types, all colors. He kind of reminds me of myself. I guess that's why we get along together so well.

Is he a left-handed Oil Can Boyd? Very much so. I would say we are each other turned inside out. Our personalities are pretty much the same, how we view life is pretty much the same. He's a very caring man for other people, very open. He's never going to be in a room and you don't know he's there. No matter what room. You could be in church and you're going to know Bill Lee is there.

He's not a character like people make him out to be, he's just eccentric. He's just Bill Lee. I like calling him "Space." I don't call him "Spaceman." "Space" is cool. I like calling him "Space." When people who don't know him call him "Spaceman," they think it's because he's a spacey person, but it's actually because he's so brilliant that he doesn't talk in the norm. He doesn't think in the norm. He's not predictable. His vast knowledge made him a really good baseball player. He could sit and think inside-out about the game and I think that's what he admired about me, too, that I love it so much because I can do it so well. We're the same that way. Right now, at 65 years old, he could walk out there in the major leagues and he could do what Jamie Moyer did.

And he could still cover first. He could do it all, right now, because he's one that talks about the science—that's why me and him talk about the game. You know, if you could only throw a ball up there at 20 mph, but you knew how to throw behind it at five mph, you can get people out.

◆ ◆ ◆

When I first got to the major league camp with the Red Sox they gave me No. 23. When I signed I didn't know a lot about the history of the Red Sox or anything. I didn't know about all the tradition and the Red Sox–Yankees rivalry. And I didn't know about the other No. 23: Louis Tiant. I didn't watch a lot of baseball because I was always *playing* baseball. Sure I'd heard of Luis Tiant and I had seen that windup of his on TV.

They gave me his number and told me that the only man who could wear this number was me. I met him in spring training '84. We sat and talked; he thought the world of me and he still does.

Some people says he's a borderline Hall of Famer. That's crazy. He's not a borderline Hall of Famer—he's a Hall of Famer! I've seen his numbers—the endurance, all the games he's won. My man's a Hall of Famer. He was an amazing pitcher. The way he was crafty was a lot like the way I tried to pitch.

He calls me his son. That always makes me feel good.

◆ ◆ ◆

There was this pitcher named Mike Brown who came up with the Red Sox at the same time as me. 1983 was one of the years that I felt like I should have made the big-league team out of spring training. I feel like Mike Brown wasn't the pitcher I was, but he was the chosen one. Mind you, that was another thing that led me to feel the way that I felt in Major League Baseball, because it was all personal to me. I was sensitive and serious about what I did and about my ability. I didn't want anybody getting the chance to pitch before me for any reason other than that they could out-pitch me, not politics. Hell, I'm better than you so I should be playing.

That's the way I felt about it. I felt like the Red Sox were biased toward him because he'd been a big prospect out of Clemson University. There was a lot of hype for this kid, but he was a piece of shit baseball player, and I didn't think much better of him as a person. He didn't even want to be my roommate when I first came to the major leagues. I guess they say it was because I smoked cigarettes, but I don't think that's the real reason.

• • •

We called Gary Allenson "Mugsy!" He caught my first major league win.

He came to the dugout and said that I was throwing 87 mph sliders. He said he hadn't ever caught sliders that hard. My slider and my fastball weren't that much different; I just put a little cut on the slider. I crossed him up the entire game, though, because I couldn't see. I told the team what the problem was with the signals and the next day they sent me to the doctor.

But, anyway, Gary complemented me when I came to the major leagues. He enjoyed catching me. He liked my spark on the mound. He was another teammate who talked to me quite a bit. He was a good dude. When I came up he was sharing the catching time with Rich Gedman and a few other guys in there.

I didn't notice Mugsy hanging with any of the cliques, but every now and then I would notice that he would run with Steamer or Shag Crawford or Mark Clear. I always thought that what they had in common was cowboy boots. All the guys who wore the cowboy boots seemed to hang together.

But overall Mugsy was a good catcher. He helped me quite a bit, and he complimented everything that I did on the mound. He was definitely good with me.

• • •

I admired Mike Greenwell's ability. I admired the way he hit. He was from the South, but he was a different kind of Southern kid, being from Florida as opposed to Alabama or Mississippi, which is a bit different. He was real free spirited and happy-go-lucky, but he had a temper. We called him Gator.

He didn't take any shit. He was serious about the game, and if you challenged him in any kind of way he wasn't afraid to tell you he'd drop you on your head. He was a redneck kid, but not a racist redneck kid. He was just a backwoods Southern kid—but he loved some Oil Can Boyd.

We were close. I was just a couple years older than he was, and I took to him right away, because he would talk to me. He wasn't standoffish at all.

He was an above-average baseball player. Didn't have blazing speed; didn't have a great arm; didn't have great pop, but he had good pop, maybe he hit 22 home runs once, but he drove in more than 90 runs a couple times. He was a lifetime .300 hitter and he did it for more than 10 years.

For a good 10-year span, he was a good ballplayer. He played the wall pretty well. See, he wasn't flashy and he didn't have that type of ego. If he had an ego, he would've been noticed. If he'd talked a little bit more about himself, he would've been noticed. Ballplayers talk about themselves—that's what I like about Dustin Pedroia. Pedroia isn't afraid to tell you that he's going to go 4-for-4, that he's going to hit lasers all over, steal eight bases, and catch everything hit near him. That's the kind of ballplayer I like to play with.

But Gator did come to me. He hated that I got upset about not being picked for the All-Star Game. I didn't know how personally he took it until the next year when he came to me in the clubhouse one day at the beginning of the season and said, "You go out this year and pitch just like you did last year, and if those son of a bitches don't pick you again, don't worry about."

He told me he didn't want me having a fit about what I couldn't control. "Don't worry about it," he said.

But in '88, when he had his best year and finished second in the MVP voting, he was singing a different tune. He said he wanted the trophy because some people were saying that Canseco was taking steroids. Canseco was blasting baseballs all over the moon. But, I'm sorry, he was 40/40 and I don't think steroids made him run 40 times. And right now, I don't know if he still takes steroids, but he still can hit a ball 800 feet. I've seen him do it out in Arizona. He'll lose the ball.

Jimmy Rice didn't take it well when Gator came. It's just part of the game. It's almost time for you to be leaving when somebody else is coming in. I would bet that Carl Yastrzemski felt the same way about Jimmy, and Ted Williams felt it when Yaz came. Life moves on, man.

Anyway, Gator was a good dude. He wife was real sweet. I knew he was a good man when he named his son after Bo Jackson. Gator loved Bo Jackson. He was as redneck as they come, but he was a good dude. Some of my best friends in the game were from the South, because they understood me.

Mike Smithson—you couldn't get a better guy. Sammy Stewart—can't get a better guy. Wes Gardner—can't get a better guy. And all of them were raised in the bigoted South. Most likely, in the era we're talking about, their parents were prejudiced. But these were guys who took the time to get to know a person. These guys knew about racism, they grew up in it and it was something they had to come to terms with. So then they come up to the major leagues and it turns out it's the kid from California who's the biggest racist. It's the kid from Illinois or Massachusetts, but not the kid from Alabama.

• • •

I grew to like Bob Stanley a little, but I don't know that I've ever forgiven him for the way he treated me when I first got there.

Throughout our time together he grew to respect how good a ballplayer I was and what type of person I was. It kind of changed his way with me. He started to compliment me and it was sincere, and I guess I wasn't man enough to let it be. He made me mad, goddamnit, and a part of me still feels like he shined the light on me right when I got there. I felt like after that there was this sense of, "Watch him." I was more upset that night that Bob and I got into it than I was when I didn't make the All-Star team, so that tells you how mad I was.

It wasn't anything specific. He didn't call me a nigger or anything like that. He just...he made me so mad.

We were in Cleveland after I'd just come up. It was my first road trip and I was kind of feeling my way a little bit. I was excited about the whole big league thing, but I felt lonely and distant, because the people I got called up with I wasn't even close to. I didn't know Marty or Chico or Marc Sullivan that well. I knew Sully in Double A but I didn't run with him. Playing with someone and running with them are two different things.

I was in the bullpen that night and Geddy was warming me up. I was told to get up and throw a bullpen session. I wasn't going in the game or anything, just getting my work in. I don't even think a coach came down there. I don't remember anybody standing behind me. I don't remember any assistance. Then, as I'm warming up, Bob Stanley started making comments. It wasn't terrible, it was just teasing. I'd throw the ball and he'd joke about how they'd seen that before, or so-and-so used to throw that. Just teasing me, you know.

But you don't know me. I ain't one of them boys. In order for you to tease me you got to know me. We just met and you're coming at me harsh. You don't even know my last name. All you know is here's this pitcher that we heard is real good and he's got this big personality.

I have my own unique way of pitching, my own flamboyant way of warming up, and he didn't like it. He's watching me, saying stuff about "What's this? What's that?" I'm just warming up. This is the first time I'd ever thrown a ball in the big leagues and he's riding me. He was so focused on me he wasn't even watching the game.

So I had to step off the rubber and say to him, "Man, leave me the fuck alone. I'm trying to get my goddamn work in."

So then he says something about this rookie popping off, and I told him it was only because he wouldn't leave me alone.

I can understand some hazing—putting shaving cream in the phone or giving me a hotfoot—but not personal, not coming at me the way he did. I felt like he was belittling me. He didn't do something to make guys laugh. It wasn't a joke because nobody was laughing at me. And nobody saw when I came off the mound and told him to leave me alone. It wasn't an atmosphere where he was trying to have fun with me, because if that was it I wouldn't have cared. I got the best sense of humor. I'm not hard to make laugh at all.

It wasn't about that.

Even Reid Nichols caught onto it. He told Bob that the only reason he was messing with me was that he was jealous. Reid was in the bullpen. He was the utility outfielder and he warmed up Jimmy between innings. Reid recognized what was going on and he hollered, "Steamer, leave him alone. Can't you see you're upsetting him?" He saw me get angry. But so did Bob, and the more I got angry the more he kept going. He heard Reid and he just kept right on messing with me. I think he was getting mad because here was this young black rookie and I wouldn't let him disrespect me. I've always thought it was racial. That was the way I took it.

So we got on the bus to leave after the game and were about to fist fight—because he didn't stop even when we got on the bus. It didn't stop until we got back to Fenway Park, off the plane! And when I got off the plane and came back in the clubhouse I was mad. I had tears in my eyes. I told Bob, "Man, if you don't leave me alone I will hurt you and I'm not fucking around with you. You don't know me and I want you to understand, I don't care if you weigh two hundred and something pounds. I got 12 brothers, so you better understand what you're dealing with—I'm a country boy."

I hadn't wanted to bring this kind of impression. I didn't want any of this—but that man wasn't going to talk to me like that, and that was that.

Then Ralph Houk called me in his office. He told me that Bob just joked around like that. That's the way he was.

I told Ralph to his face, "If you're going to defend the way this man's talking to me, Sir, I don't have no goddamn respect for you," and I walked out of his office.

That's why ever since then things started changing. That night changed my whole life in the game of baseball, all the way up until today. First day of me playing was the last day of me playing. That right there made it to where I would always be looked at, because the way I acted and the things I said got into the guts of certain people. I was not messing around. I told Bob Stanley right then, "I don't care if I play another day, if you fuck with me like that again, you're going to the motherfucking emergency room," and I meant that.

So when this happened, that's when people kind of started being like, "Heeeeee might snap." Now they knew a different side of me, and not the one that I wanted seen when I came to the major leagues. I had fights in the minor leagues and I didn't want that to carry up there with me. Then, as soon as I came up, here's a man 240 pounds sizing me up. He was teasing me about how small I was, but that night everyone learned that I was a little dog with a big old bite.

So at that point I became very defensive. From that point on, if anybody came to me with any kind of comment or joke that I thought might be disrespectful I became very defensive. I took everybody like Steamer. It might not have been right but that's what I did. It doesn't matter if it was Wade or Glenn Hoffman or Mark Clear or Shag, in my mind it was always to the extreme. That's why people would say, "Damn, why's he having these temper tantrums, these fits?" It was almost like my blood would boil, and then I felt alone. Not a lot of the guys would stick up for me. Jimmy, for instance, never said a word. Dewey would though. He'd tell Steamer and them to leave me alone. It'd stop for a while, but it wouldn't go away.

Also, in my opinion, Steamer was a brownnoser. Steamer was a guy who sucked up to the press, so they wouldn't write bad stuff about him. I also think he sucked up to the coaches and the managers so he could have his way and be the way he wanted to be, and Ralph Houk and them let him do that.

• • •

The whole thing with Julio Valdez and the statutory rape arrest was scary, because a lot of people might have been involved with that girl. She was a white girl who said that she was 17. She looked like she was 19 or 20, body like a grown-ass lady. She had a reputation with the ballplayers. Still, a lot of players thought she might be lying about her age. No matter how she dressed or anything, she had a baby face.

I heard that a lot of guys on the visitors' teams were with her, because they could hit it and get away. Then she started turning her attention to the home team and to the minor league team in Pawtucket. I heard a story that she came to an apartment house and nine or ten guys did her. Now I don't know if Julio was one of them, or if he was with her at a different time, or if he never met her before in his life, but I know it was Julio who got busted for statutory rape. Turns out she was only 14.

Apparently she went home and her dad started asking questions, because I guess he'd heard rumors, and the next thing you know the police were taking Julio away in handcuffs from the dugout during a game.

I can tell you, there were a lot of nervous people when that happened.

Eventually, though, the grand jury failed to indict and the charges were dropped. He was just a young shortstop at the time, and I still don't know today why she picked him. I don't think he ever played one day after that. He didn't even go to the minors. But he was a coach for a long time.

◆ ◆ ◆

Marc Sullivan was Haywood Sullivan's son. He was cool. I came up with Marc, playing in the minors with him. He caught me pretty much every day in Double A, and then a little bit in Triple A. We also played in the major leagues together. Sully was cool, and I got a chance to know his family real well. His dad was a big-league catcher.

His dad, Haywood, managed Satchel Paige in 1965. He told me about it. His dad really liked me a lot. He thought a hell of a lot of me as a pitcher and as a person. He was from the South, so he kind of knew what I was about. He didn't really bother me with what people would say or anything. He was pretty much on my side, because his kids loved me. Haywood was cool. He gave me an opportunity to play for his team.

Marc made it in the big leagues, too. He could throw. I just think that Marc was there at the wrong time; too many good young players at his position. Rich Gedman was younger than he was and Geddy had been to the big league a couple years before. Geddy had made his way in the majors and the Red Sox had their sights set on Geddy at catcher.

Sully was all right, and he was very baseball oriented. I always thought that he'd be a manager one day. He was working in the Texas Rangers organization the last that I heard but that was a long time ago.

Marc couldn't hit real well. He could catch, but he didn't have a very good stick. He was long-legged like his daddy. But he was all right. He was the one I crossed up all night that one time in Double A, the one who went and told the manager, "Dennis needs glasses," and I was at the doctor the next day.

As far as the glasses, I didn't like pitching with them. I never liked pitching with the frames on. Still today I pitch with the naked eye. I just felt more comfortable. I had problems in the nighttime, but day games were fine. I tried to wear contacts and they would stick to my eyeballs, which made everything real blurry, so it was back to nothing.

• • •

They called George Scott "Boomer." He wasn't a teammate, having come before me, but I knew about him when I was playing at Jackson State. I knew that he had come from Greenville, Mississippi. We always had this magazine in the South called *Hometown Heroes* that showed all the kids from the South that were playing professional ball. It had been around for a long time and in the '70s we saw George Scott in there. They would tell about Boo Ferriss being down at Delta State, and my brothers, and a bunch of other kids from Mississippi.

Kelvin Moore, who played at Jackson State University with me and then played professionally, loved George Scott. I remember hearing a pro scout talk about him while I was still in college. He said Boomer was hitting balls across the highway. This scout said he was a massive black man, and he said he had the nicest hands in the world. The scout nicknamed him "Black Beauty," and it was all he could talk about: George Scott, George Scott, George Scott.

The Pride of the Delta. It was almost like we knew him, when I was a kid growing up, just because he was from home. That just shows you how proud black people were in the South. They thought highly about black athletes who would go off and prosper, from me to Walter Payton to *all* of them. From Lem Barney to everybody that has come through there—Robert Brazile, Purvis Short, Lindsey Hunter—we're proud of all the guys the South produces, as well as the white athletes who came out, including Archie Manning and his kids.

It was real good knowing that George Scott was making a big name up in Boston. That's the first time we'd ever heard that a black man was playing in Beantown. "What the hell is *Bean*-town? What you talking about, Bean-town?" "Hey man, that's where those white folks landed on Plymouth Rock up there." It was a history lesson all in one. To me, growing up, Boston might as well have been on the other side of the world. We didn't know. I remember thinking it must get colder than hell up there and people talk funny up there and are there any black folk up there? "Yeah, man, there's black people up there."

We didn't know. We thought all the damn black people in the country were in the South. We thought the other states had no black people. We thought all of them were here because where I grew up it was 85 percent black. We knew most of the United States was white, so it just sort of made sense.

So here's a black man, George Scott, we can pull for, playing for the Boston Red Sox. That's when we would hear the name Carl Yastrzemski. You'd go to the little league ballpark or the nearest sporting goods store and you'd see the names burned on the bat. When we were little it seemed like the same three all the time: Pete Rose, Carl Yastrzemski, Mickey Mantle.

When I was growing up, I used to hit with a "Pete Rose" 30. Then we hit with the "Mickey Mantle" and then we had a "Jackie Robinson" and then we had a "Nelson Fox." Everybody had bats back then. Reggie Jackson had his name on a bat that one of the kids had in little league, but still most of the bats were Rose, Yastrzemski, or Mickey Mantle. Believe it or not, growing up as a kid, I never saw Willie Mays or Hank Aaron on a single bat.

Like I said, I hit with a "Pete Rose" 30. So it was crazy to grow up and play with and against these guys. I remember looking at Pete Rose and thinking, *Damn, I was hitting with your bat at nine years old and I'm facing you in spring training in '83.*

• • •

I played baseball with Michael Jordan with the White Sox in spring training in '95, when they were planning on using replacement players. This was before the strike ended and the regular players came back. Michael's locker was right next to mine. Every morning, we would talk a little bit. Michael's quiet. Walter Hriniak, the hitting coach, introduced us. When I first got there, Walter came walking over with Michael Jordan and said, "Dennis, he wants to meet you."

175

I shook his hand. I said, "What's up, Shoes?" I called him "Shoes" because the motherfucker's got shoes named after him, you know. He would have been a pretty fine little baseball player if he stayed with it, because he was a real good athlete. He had good hands, he just had a lot to learn. He didn't know the techniques of playing all the time. Some people said he was rusty. That's crazy. You ain't ever played, how can you be rusty? Little league don't count. He jumped right into minor league ball and he hadn't ever played before. That's an athlete.

◆ ◆ ◆

Bill Fischer was one of my pitching coaches with the Red Sox and I loved him. Fisch is one of a kind. First of all, he had a great sense of humor and he was a real nice man.

He became the Red Sox pitching coach in '85 when John McNamara brought him with him. I really didn't know of him as a pitcher in the major leagues, but he would tell great stories about his career. He often told the story about the time he gave up a 507-foot home run to Mickey Mantle.

He knew the game. He complimented us as pitchers *and* as men—me especially—and he had a unique way with all of us on the staff. He was an individual's pitching coach. He treated everyone differently. He knew how to adjust to different kinds of personalities.

He and I had a lot of things in common, like cigarettes for instance. It was funny, I would come off of the mound and we would often share a cigarette. Usually he'd have one lit for me already, and we'd share a smoke and discuss the game. It was cool. I would come down the steps and he'd be in the tunnel with a cigarette waiting for me, and he'd say, "Atta boy, Can, that's what I'm talking about. Get that bender working. Get that big one working and you'll be all right tonight. Keep the ball down, work them."

Basically my whole career in the major leagues I smoked cigarettes in the dugout. It wasn't like it is today: no smoking on the premises or in the whole damn ballpark.

I'll never forget, one day I came up to the tunnel and I was smoking a cigarette at the top of the steps and I got caught on camera. I'm standing right there with John McNamara and I'm just smoking away before I go back out to the mound. I was blowing smoke up into the air as I ran on out to the mound.

That's not the worst, though. One night in Boston I was smoking a cigarette and I was so intense and so focused on the ballgame that I walked out to the mound with a lit cigarette in my hand. I forgot I had it and walked out to the mound, but when I got across the line I looked down and I was like, "Goddamn." So I called the clubhouse boy out and gave it to him. I said, "Take this over there and put it out. Don't throw it away because I'll be back." I'd just fire it up when I got back.

I always kept my pack of cigarettes in the tunnel, along with my matches or lighter and a chair. I'd sit in there and the guys would walk by when they had to go to the bathroom or run back to the clubhouse. It didn't matter which stadium we were at, I always set up my cigarettes and my chair in the tunnel.

Fischer was great with all of the little things I needed to be happy and comfortable. He was very unique. He knew that I had a good sense of humor and he could make me laugh with a lot of crazy stuff that he would say.

One day I was warming up in the bullpen and he was real animated. "Bring it here! You're throwing like a mashed potato. Bring it here, Can." No catcher ever caught us. He caught us every day. Roger, me, Bruce, all of us—he warmed us all up, with this old mitt from back in the day. It just had a pocket. It didn't have any webbing or anything, it was just this primitive thing that should have been in a baseball museum. It didn't really matter, though. He had hands that looked like gloves themselves. "C'mon, you don't weigh but 150 pounds," he said, "throw it all up here. Throw your hat up here, too. Throw everything!" So I reared back and fired it up there and he dropped his mitt and caught that ball barehanded. I'm throwing 90 and he just snatched it out of the air with his bare hand.

"You have to have a better one than that," he said. "Throw me a real fastball!"

I was laughing so hard, I couldn't believe what I saw. He caught my four-seamer barehanded! I'm like, "Fisch, I just threw this ball as hard as I can."

I told Roger, "The man is a monster. The man is an alien."

We'd be doing our conditioning in the outfield and sometimes, as we were running by, he'd say some of the funniest things you ever heard. "Don't you go out and get too drunk tonight," and all kinds of stuff. "Hey, I know you're going to be out chasing women tonight. Well, make sure you don't catch nothing. I don't want to see anybody with balls this big tomorrow." So he's saying crazy stuff like this when you're running by him, and if you didn't know him you wouldn't know what to think, but the truth is he's just the sweetest man.

He and John McNamara were both good to me. There weren't many times that McNamara had to come out to the mound and ask for the ball from me. Fisch would come out to the mound and do the visit, or McNamara would come out just to talk to me. I liked that better than the managers today who just send out the pitching coach. I want to talk to the skipper—he's the one who's going to come out here and take the damn ball. John Mac would come out to the mound just to talk to me, because we had a real good relationship.

Fisch would come out there every now and then and make me laugh when I needed it. He would come out to the mound because he knew I got mad as hell when I gave up a home run or a couple runs. (I was never a player to get all animated and angry when there was a botched play behind me. I don't think it's right when pitchers do that. I would never want that done to me. They're giving you a great effort and they're major leaguers. Believe me, if it can be caught most times they'll catch it. Nine out of 10 times. That's why they're major leaguers.) So, Fisch used to come out to the mound after I gave up a home run or something and I was steaming mad. I'd walk behind the mound, taking about 10 to 20 seconds before I'd go back and throw the next pitch. Those were the times when I'd see Mac gesture to him—*go talk to him, see if he's all right out there.*

So Fisch would come out, all relaxed. "Can, take a deep breath. You see that scoreboard? You just gave up a home run, right?"

I'd say, "Yeah."

"That run is never going to come down," he said. "It's going to be up there for 2,000 years. It's never going to come down so you can forget about it."

I started laughing on the mound, and he'd come back around and give me a smile before going back and he knew I was all right. He got my mind off of boiling out there and wanting to kill everybody.

Sometimes he'd come out if I didn't get mad after giving up some runs. He'd say, "What's wrong? You're not angry. You're not mad. This must be another guy out here—I don't know who this is. We need Oil Can out here. You can send that other guy back in the dugout. Go find that crazy son of a bitch and get him out here."

He would say something like that and I'd realize that it was time for me to get intense. And automatically I could change my whole character and personality. I could always change real quick. Sometimes it would happen in between pitches, just because a guy swung at a pitch real hard and I felt like he was trying to blast my shit away and rub it in or something. I could change right in the middle of an at-bat and go at a guy real hard, all because I could see on his face that's he's intense. I would react to Eddie Murray's attitude in the batter's box, or I would react to Reggie Jackson's attitude in the batter's box. Certain ballplayers came to the plate and I could tell that they wanted to hit my shit to the moon, they couldn't wait to knock it out so they could walk around the bases and show me up.

That was the good part of playing baseball for me. I was very noticeable to the opponent, more so probably than any other pitcher in my period in time. Maybe Dave Stieb was close. He had a temper on the mound. He'd get hot and slam the ball in his glove and walk behind the mound and throw some F-bombs, saying all kinds of things and basically freaking out because he hung a slider or grooved a fastball. He was pretty much like me, too, in that a hard-hit ball off of him would wake him up. Something unexpected in an inning would give a guy like me or Dave Stieb a little bit of added motivation on the mound. Temper and attitude were part of our toolbox.

Bill Fischer said to me that John McNamara would include me in the top five pitchers he ever managed. The man was around the game for almost 50 years, so that made me feel real good. I felt similarly when Luis Tiant said that I could pitch anywhere. He said that just a couple years ago. He tried to get me signed with an independent team. A couple teams actually called me, because I threw the ball so well, and Luis said that I could probably pitch in the major leagues right now. And I *know* I can. It's called pitching, not throwing, because it's a skill, and for guys like me it doesn't go away with age. I would've loved to have seen myself out there like Dennis Eckersley, pitching in the major leagues at

43, or like Wakefield, but not throwing a trick pitch. No, I don't want to rely on a knuckleball, but just a great mind, great science, knowing that no matter how hard I throw, every ball is different to every batter.

• • •

I didn't have much of a relationship with Lou Gorman. There was just no personal connection; he was the GM and I was the player. I don't know if other ballplayers got to talk with the GM, on contracts or whatever, but I didn't have many run-ins with him. He spoke highly of me, but I don't think that he and my agent liked each other. I'd been having some problems with my agent, but I'd stuck with him up to that point.

Lou was straight with me and he didn't want me to leave and go to Montreal. He had told me, back in '84 or '85, that I could pitch in Boston for 10 years easy.

I always thought that a bunch of the info I was getting on other agents and stuff might be coming down from Lou, but I could never be sure. It even came from Jim Rice one time. My old agent and I had gone our separate ways, and this was right when Jimmy came to talk to me. That was how I got to be with the new agents, and I'm thankful to Jimmy for that to this day. It helped me and Karen a lot when we were young, switching to IMG, and it was Jimmy who turned me on to IMG, who he was with.

Lou stood in there for me through a lot of stuff. When I got hurt he kind of had to deal with me differently. I think he would have paid me the money that I would've earned had I not been hurt in '87, '88, and '89, but I think his hand was forced, what with him still being under Mrs. Yawkey. Their view seemed to be that when I wasn't healthy I pretty much didn't deserve to be rewarded. I had to do a 100-percent job. I couldn't be like some of these pitchers you see today, pitching half-assed and making money.

• • •

I loved John Tudor. Man, I loved Tooty. He wasn't there long enough, but I still do functions for him all the time now. He was very down-to-earth with me. He didn't jump on the bandwagon. He was very different than Bob Stanley and a lot of those guys. He was cool for the time I was there with him.

Bobby Ojeda was kind of in that clique with Steamer and them. I think he was caught in a sort of identity conflict, too. I've heard Jose Canseco say it before. He said that for the most part he was considered white, but he was Cuban, so he was a little different. There's a fear that comes with that, a feeling that you're on the edge of fitting in, so you don't want to do anything to make trouble. I think Bobby Ojeda had that same phobia. That's the way I looked at it, so I didn't really have a good relationship with Bobby, just on that, because he wanted to treat me like they did and I wasn't allowing that.

And believe it or not, I underestimated him in the World Series. He was one of those guys who complained about pitching in Fenway with the Green Monster looming over there. Lefties complained about that wall a lot. "It's hard to keep the ball off the wall. I can't pitch in this ballpark." Bobby Ojeda was one of the guys who carried on, so I thought the intimidation of pitching in Fenway Park would get him, but it didn't.

Bruce Hurst could pitch at Fenway, because Bruce didn't mind pitching inside. Bruce would throw the ball up under your chin and then get you out with his change-up. But it's hard for any lefty to pitch in there. I'm sorry, I just didn't see

Bobby Ojeda as being tough. I just didn't. I underestimated his personality—not his pitching, his personality, before Game 3.

He was there with me from '82 through '85, so he got to know me a little bit. You know what shocked those guys most of all, though? It was my intellect. That's where they eventually realized that they weren't messing with no Stepin Fetchit–type brother from the South like others they'd known.

So they had this image that if you were from the South you would be this certain way. I was totally opposite of what they said.

• • •

Brian Cole was the top prospect in the Mets organization. He was a center fielder, and my mama and his daddy were first cousins, so we were cousins. He was killed in a car accident in Florida in '01. It was a sad day for my family.

The original story said Brian was thrown from the car because he wasn't wearing a seat belt, and how a seatbelt saved his passenger, who was hardly hurt.

The Ford Motor Company settled with the family after a judgment of $131 million because the jury ruled that Brian was wearing a seatbelt but it didn't operate properly. Obviously, the settlement was based on what a star prospect might have made in the future.

It was in 2001, and looking it up on the Internet, I found that the family's lawyer said, "He was just a wonderful kid. As Jim Duquette stated, they were building the team around him. He was a remarkable athlete. He was going to be a superstar. Jim and the Mets organization pegged him with Torii Hunter and [Jose] Reyes. They had him pegged with all those types of guys. His numbers were as good."

He was a special talent and a special kid.

183

• • •

Don Slaught was a gamer. On May 17, 1986, at a game at Fenway Park, I threw a pitch that hit him in his face, breaking his nose and his cheekbone. It's important to me that people understand that I wasn't trying to hit Don on purpose. I ain't ever tried to hit a ballplayer. But me hitting Don, that's why the canvas is over the center-field seats. They said that Don lost the ball in the sunlight. I did hear rumors that people told him that he had to stop diving out over the plate, because he was going to get hurt one day.

He had fouled off a couple sliders that were a foot or so outside. He dove out and poked them into the visitors dugout. He was really not giving me much respect, so I threw a fastball inside to back him off the plate, but he got hit and hurt pretty bad. Then it got around the league that I was a head hunter and everything. But even all his teammates knew that I wasn't trying to hurt him.

I still feel really bad about it. Actually, I didn't pitch real well for a while after because I had it in my mind that I had almost killed a guy. It really affected me, seeing him come out to the ballpark with the whole face mask thing on. But he was a gamer, man. He played for a long time, and he was a real good ballplayer. I had big respect for him, how he jumped right back in the batters box and wasn't ball shy. He came back in and played his career out.

• • •

When things were at their worst I met a lot of good people. One of the best was this lawyer named Ronald Michaels. He's still involved in my life today, because he took up the case the federal government had against me.

To this day he still says that he doesn't know how I landed on his doorstep like a lost puppy, because out of nowhere I was in his life. Well, the way I met him was that my wife had left me and I was with Renita, who I mentioned earlier. Me and Karen were separated and, hell, I needed some kind of companionship. I still needed somebody to cook for me and clean for me. Maybe I'm selfish, but I have to have that. But then, out of nowhere, Renita died of an aneurysm.

Pretty much right then I didn't care about God; I didn't care about nobody. I didn't really care about how I was living or how my morals were or anything like that. That was when I met Ronald. Ronald happened to be a religious man, and he tried to bring me closer to God. I didn't want to accept it, but Ronald stayed after me.

Looking back, Ronald was somebody that God put into my life. Now I'm real close with him, with his wife and his kids, his nieces and nephews, his mom, his family. I know a lot about his life. He's a white guy who grew up hearing about how being segregated was good. He lived in a world that taught that God is white and all that stuff. He grew up like that. But when I met him he told me a different story.

There's a difference between growing up surrounded by racism and growing up *in* racism. His family was different. His great-great-granddad or whatever fought in the Civil War—for the *North*! This was a man from Tupelo, Mississippi! Ronald knew everything that came out of my mind and mouth was about black and white, so this was hard for me to grasp.

He said, "I want to show you something, Dennis. Come in the parlor." And there, on the wall of a white man's home in Mississippi, is a civil war uniform. But it ain't gray. It's blue.

I said, "That's the North, Ronald."

Ronald told me that some long-dead relative of his was rebellious, and when the war started he joined the North. He switched uniforms with a dead soldier.

And I'm like, "If that ain't the coolest shit I ever heard ..."

So we got to know each other quite well. In the process, I was very honest with him. He knew I wanted to be a businessman—wanted to be a black businessman. He knew what being a black businessman meant to me. The whole idea of it is profoundly annoying to lots of rich white people down South. For a black man to want to own anything is a sort of insult to them. "You're supposed to be owned, not own stuff." That's the mentality.

When I first met Ronald I had a business proposal with me which I had spent $36,000 to do. It was done by some experts, some big-time college professors. They sat me down and found out I was very sharp in business. They asked me what I was planning to do and they put together all the facts and figures. I was knowledgeable about what I wanted to do, and they put it together for me. They charged me a fine mint for the proposal, and along with the blueprints for the stadium and everything else, it cost me about $70,000. Then, of course, I'd spent the money to develop the property for the ballfield, which was over a quarter of a million dollars. At that time I was just watching all this money go down the drain.

I was telling Ronald Michaels about these things, and believe it or not he already knew. He was from Mississippi and he'd heard. I think everybody in the state knew if a black man in Mississippi was spending that kind of money. I mean, even though I was 100 miles away from home, this lawyer had heard what I'd been up to.

He knew that the banks had turned me away. And we both thought we knew why they did, too. They tried to make it look like I wasn't viable, but that's not so. I didn't come in there asking for money; I came in there putting up money for money. I was using my own money. But in my opinion they used my childhood and my family's childhood and the things that I'd said and the animosity that they'd kept for 20 years. Because ever since I signed a professional contract, and even when I went to Jackson State, I often talked about my hometown, and it wasn't positive. Hell, in the minor leagues I was ashamed to tell people I was from Mississippi. I would tell them I was from Louisiana. It seemed like it was better. Sometimes I'd tell people I was from Tennessee. Basically, once I got to the major leagues it didn't matter.

I would even tell ballplayers who were from Mississippi that I was from somewhere else. We'd be together and someone would say, "I'm from Jackson, Mississippi," and I would still say, "I'm from Monroe, Louisiana." And more than once they were like, "Man, Dennis, you know you from Meridian, Mississippi." I never knew what to say. I was ashamed, because people had preconceived ideas if they knew you were from a place like Meridian. They either thought that you were ignorant and that you'd been walked all over, that you could be intimidated, or they thought that you were angry and out of control.

These are the things that Ronald Michaels and I would talk about. He'd ask me about my whole major league career, where I'd been and where I'd gone. I told him about how I felt like I had been banished from the game of baseball (and I even have an attorney today who's looking into that). It all happened in a round-about way. I think drugs just gave people a reason to shun me. They were going to do it anyway; the drugs just gave them a reason.

I was in the right frame of mind then and I was praying to my God. I started to realize some of the things I wanted in life. I want true equality in people. I want people to be able to look at people and appreciate the difference in people. I want people to see what's different and what's cool about life. Feeling that way may seem real naïve in this world. I know in some ways it made me very naïve and passive and easy. I truly believe that what I'm trying to do in this book is make people see and understand that true equality is letting people believe what they want to believe, letting them live how they want to live, within the means of not hurting anybody. Culture difference is the coolest shit. If you're a person who supposedly "loves God so much," how can you not recognize the good and quit trying to find the bad in everybody, creating vice and strife out in the world.

But even while I know how I want to live, I'm still mad as hell that I wasn't allowed to pitch 20 years in the major leagues. I can't let go of that anger.

I took it very personally when Bill Fischer told me that I was going to pitch as long as I wanted to pitch. He said, "You'll pitch as long as you want to pitch." He said that I knew—*truly knew*—how to pitch when I was only 23 or 24 years old, and as I got older and kept learning I was just going to get better. That's what burns so much. If they hadn't forced me out, what could I have been?

◆ ◆ ◆

In 1982, I had one of the best seasons that you could have in minor league baseball. I went out and threw the ball very well in Bristol, Connecticut, and I was promoted to the major leagues in September.

My first day up in the big leagues, that's something I'll always remember. I woke up at the Sheraton Hotel in Boston and just thought, I'm in *The Show*! I walked out of the hotel, getting ready to catch a cab, and standing right there was Lou Whitaker. He was waiting for a cab, too, so I introduced myself and shook his hand.

And just to the right of me was a little Asian kid by the name of Norman Yee. I didn't know at that time that Norman and I would go on to become very good friends. Actually, he was the first Asian person I'd ever spent a lot of time with.

I was intrigued. Mind you, I grew up loving martial arts movies, and I still watch them a lot today. Every chance I get I watch martial arts movies. I have about 100 martial arts and kung fu movies. I'm very intrigued about Asian culture and martial artists' ability to do the things that they do. A lot of that started, of course, with the whole Bruce Lee thing.

In Mississippi, there were no Asian people when I grew up. There who only black people, white people, and a few Indians out on a reservation. But other than that there were no other races or cultures, so I was very intrigued when I met Norman. And Norman and I are very close to this day.

From that first day I met him, I felt very passionately about him as a friend. He went on all my road trips and everything throughout my entire major league career. He even helped me work on this book. And Norman wasn't the only one who was good to me. His mom and dad, his whole family, they were so good to me. His mom couldn't speak any English, and when I would call the house and ask for him his mom would say, "Oh, Norman no here." But she knew it was me on the phone. His mom and dad are very sweet people. I think his mom might speak a little bit of English now, but his dad speaks a lot of English. As I was in the process of writing this book Norman's father was having some health problems and it's my hope that maybe I can get a copy sent to him in Chinese. I'd like to be able to tell him in his own language how close his son has been to me and how he's stuck by me through everything.

Norman knows a lot of the teammates who I've been close to over the years, like Delino DeShields and Marquis Grissom. He got to know a bunch of different ballplayers, because everywhere I went he was with me and everybody was intrigued. *Who's this Chinese kid running around with Dennis?* Everyone just got to know him as one of my closest friends.

He's been with me my whole baseball life and beyond, and I'm very grateful to have a friend like that. There was no time I've ever called on him that he wasn't there for me, and he always treated me with great respect. He never like, brownnosed. He got to know me real close and he got to talk to me like a brother. He has always been there to tell me the dos and don'ts, the wills and won'ts, and he's always there to say, "You shouldn't be this way. You shouldn't do that. Don't try this. Don't do that. I'll help you with this. I'll help you with that, but don't do this." That's the way Norman was with me, and that's the way he is today. I couldn't leave him out in this book of my life.

• • •

In 1983, Lou Whitaker helped me out a hell of a lot, probably more than any ballplayer in the major leagues. He just said one simple thing to me. Lou said, "You throw too many strikes. You've got to stay away from the plate more, and you'll be all right." And from that day on, I turned into a full-fledged pitcher. Everything that Lou told me, I did. And I'm really thankful for Lou for being the man that he was and sharing his knowledge of the game with me. I'm thankful to him for helping me as a black man in the game, helping me to understand how to play this game at a major league level.

I also really appreciated getting to know Chet Lemon and Larry Herndon, too. They were real good guys. Cliff Johnson was also a really good guy with me. Mike Easler, Joe Morgan (the ballplayer), Tony Perez, Mike Torrez, all of them were great guys. I still love and idolize all of those guys today for the men that they were.

Toby Harrah was a real good man, and he said something real nice about me when he first faced me. He said that I was going to be a fine pitcher. He said he was real pleased with what he saw in the young man that the Red Sox sent to the hill in my first start in the major leagues in September '82.

So I'm very grateful for the people that I've met in the game. Paul Molitor: great hitter, great person. Gary Gaetti and Kent Hrbek: great people. And of course, my real good friend, the late Kirby Puckett—we were real close.

I met a lot of cool people in the game, and while I'm sure I'm forgetting some, none were cooler than those people I wrote about here. Regardless of whatever happened in my career an life, all of them touched me in some kind of way. And put it like this baby: I appreciate it! From the bottom of my heart!

◆ ◆ ◆

Finally, I want to talk about my loving wife, Karen. She's been the greatest. She stood by me from day one. I met her in Pawtucket, Rhode Island, in '83, and we've been together ever since. We have two kids together: Dennis II, and my daughter, Tala. They're the sweetest thing that could ever be.

We've got Southern roots, northern roots, a multitude of different kinds of folks on both sides of the family. We have the Creole culture, Cape Verdean culture, African American culture, which is really all one culture that's been created from a multitude of people, but all descendents of Africans.

My wife is real sweet. Her mom, Lorraine; her dad, Dr. Isadore Ramos; and not to mention my wife's cousins—the family that I married into was a real good. And they've been with me from day one. Sometimes they understand me, sometimes they don't. But that's okay. That has to do with a lot of cultural background, me growing up in the South and them growing up in the north. They see life one way, and I see life another way. But it came together, and we're one good family right now.

Like I said, Karen has been with me from day one, and she's still there with me through the ups and downs, my craziness, my everything, because she knows I'm a good man. She believes in what I stand for, and that's why she stood behind me. And yes, I have been a fucked-up husband at times, but I've been a great husband, too. My own personal demons caused a lot of things, but she lived through all that too.

We're going to hang in there. I'm glad that from the day that I started until the day I ended writing this book about our life, she's still there with me right now. And we're going to do what we got to do to continue our lives together. I've been through a lot of stuff, some of it pretty ugly, but the important thing is that I still have my family at the end of it all. A lot of people who went through what I've been through have probably been through three or four divorces, because life is tough. I even had a lot of teammates who gave up on their families, but I wasn't doing that, no matter what. And my family didn't give up on me, either. I'm proud of that more than anything, that I'm a married man and I love my family. My family's been with me—even my sisters and brothers and everyone—they've stood by me through things. Believe it or not, this baseball life has been real hard on family. Everybody thinks there's money and fame and everything's good. That's the last thing that it was. What I experienced was a lot of animosities and jealousy and anger and bad things said and feelings hurt. Major League Baseball broke up my family. So now that I'm not in Major League Baseball, I'm trying to put my family back together.

That's what I'm doing right now. As long as I stay around baseball though, and think about family, I'll be just fine.

10: The World According to Oil Can

"I pitched in a ballgame once in Montreal, and for five straight innings I threw a straight change-up every pitch."

The World According to Oil Can

African Americans in Baseball

I still have mixed feelings about the game of baseball. One of the main reasons is that I know that guys like Delino DeShields and myself, and several other ballplayers like us, we're more concerned with having blacks play baseball than Major League Baseball is. We're way more concerned than they are. We're way more ready to put forth an effort to do that. They might have the means and the money and all that, but it's like me and Delino always say: basically, they don't need us no more. That's what has happened.

Major League Baseball doesn't need the African American baseball player no more. When they needed him, they used him for 50 years. They created the game. They created commerce. They created revenue, and now here we have modern-day baseball. It's commercialized and they're making gazillions of dollars from sponsorships and TV revenue and all of these things that the African American helped create. And we don't benefit at all from it. No more than maybe play center field or maybe a first baseman here or there. We're just not needed.

It's almost like it's going backward! To where, at one time there was an abundance of blacks, post-Jackie Robinson, and now all of a sudden there are *no* blacks. You say, "What happened?" It's not the desire. It's not that they don't love it any more, or that they want to go play basketball or football.

To know the history of the game is to know how messed up things are now. I can't speak for Jimmy Rice. I can't speak for Willie Mays. I can't speak for any African American ballplayer who played professional baseball except myself. I know maybe at the time Willie Mays came into the major leagues, they were kind of feeling like they were *entitled*. I don't think Jackie felt like he was entitled. Jackie was just chosen to go and do something different. But the guys who came immediately after Jackie had some kind of crazy attitude. Willie Mays and Hank Aaron and those guys, I got to hear them speak as I got older, and for some reason they felt like they were entitled to be there. In a way it's kind of a sick type of feeling. It's almost a Catch-22, to where it felt like they were entitled, "Because I'm good enough to play there." But that's not the entitlement that players should be looking for, that "I'm good enough to play there."

The league knew the players were good enough to play, so they weren't proving anything by their desire to play integrated baseball. They were looking for something they already had. So what they were really saying was what you had in Negro League baseball wasn't important at all.

I experienced that attitude. It has been said to me by a black ballplayer who had played in that period in time—that they were special, they were different. I couldn't figure that out. It felt like they were saying they were special and they didn't really care about the ballplayers coming up behind them. I experienced that one-on-one with Jimmy Rice. By me being different than him, by him playing for the Boston Red Sox—maybe if he was with the St. Louis Cardinals he wouldn't have felt that way—but by him playing with the Red Sox, I feel like he quickly accepted the notion of being a token.

So when I went there, I saw that I wasn't welcome, by him more than anybody. I kind of felt like he wanted to be the only black there. I don't think he wanted anybody else of color on that team with him, because he was treated in such a way that no black man would want to be treated. If he was true to himself I think he'd see that that's become tokenized. I got there and saw that with him. It was like the big secret, and now somebody knew that he was up there kissing ass. That's the way I looked at it. Now somebody knew. The African American guys who played with him before me were like him. And I knew I was different when I got there, in attitude. I just think he didn't want any eyes on him.

It was like I was stealing his show. Here's another black guy—a very colorful and outspoken black guy—attention's going to be taken away from me. That's the way I felt; that he had been put in that position so much, that, "I'm Jim Rice," and all the guys looking at him and he's walking around there like he's some Mandingo warrior or some shit.

I never talked to him about it. I just ignored it. I tried to stay at a distance. I think that's why when I would get upset about things in the clubhouse, or somebody would say something that I didn't like, he wouldn't come to my defense, because he didn't want them to see that he cared about another black man. It's as simple as that.

I experienced that my whole life growing up. That's no different than Stepin Fetchit. That's no different than the slave and the house nigger. That's the mentality that I'm talking about. So those are the things that you get out of that. I'm treated better than that black man right there because the master likes me. He don't like him. The master likes me, so the master gives me a little bit more than he gives him. That's what happened with me in Boston. And everybody knows what happens to a renegade slave, a rebellious slave. I was looked at like I was Nat Turner.

All that filtered out from the clubhouse to the press, from the press to the public. Even today I see it. People love me when I'm out. I admire that people do respect me when I'm out, but every now and then a friend of a friend will tell me about how they have to defend me to someone else, because that other person heard that I was a racist or crazy or out of control or whatever.

I run into that all the time, where someone says, "Man, I have to defend you when I go out in the public and tell people I know you." Some people say, "I hear the sweetest things in the world about you." But others say differently.

Some people think they know you from what they've read in the newspapers. The funny thing is that I'm an open book. You only have to know me for 10 minutes and you know pretty much everything about me.

For instance, I was a great basketball player, but I did not love basketball like I loved baseball. This goes back to what I was saying about African American ballplayers. If you remember, I played ball with Michael Jordan, and I can tell you, Michael Jordan loved baseball better than basketball. He was just a better basketball player, but he loved baseball. That's because there ain't any game that's going to bring more passion to you than baseball. No game. Because baseball is a game that no one's ever really good at. That's why you'll never be challenged in any sport like you're challenged in baseball. It's designed for you to fail. Every real man wants that challenge, that he could be good at something that's designed to make him fail.

That's the problem. Right now, black kids don't understand that metaphor around the game of baseball. Nobody's telling them what the game means personally, what the game has done for those who love it. I remember this one time when I was sitting around with some of the guys in Fort Dix and we got to talking. We were having just a good old black conversation about how we messed up out here in a white man's world, just straight talk.

I asked these guys what the first corporate business African Americans had out of slavery was. I said, "Let me tell you something about the post-slavery commerce of black people in this country. What industry were we awarded in this country post-slavery? Tell me. Baseball. That was the only corporate business that we had when we got out of slavery. It was the only business that a black man had for his own."

And I said, "Jackie Robinson and nobody had the right to take that away." That was the only thing that we had to be proud of out of slavery. It wasn't just Negro League baseball—it was what we had to be proud of—that if the master didn't give us 40 acres and a mule we could still make it in this country.

Black Ownership

Everybody knows that sports make the world go 'round. Two-thirds of the athletes who are playing these sports are people of color. The NBA is 99 percent black. Black men running up and down the floor and Michael Jordan and Isiah Thomas are the only ones who tried to get into the ownership of the league. And Michael Jordan got into it because he made so much money with them they pretty much had to give him that. Mike's made so much money. They *owed* Mike that. He did too much for the NBA. He did more for the NBA than any basketball player who ever lived, and you better believe he deserved ownership in it.

Bob Johnson was an owner in Charlotte. Somebody bought BET away from him, though. They just call it Black Entertainment now; it ain't owned by blacks anymore. They bought him out, just like Famous Amos Cookies. His face is on the bag and he don't even own it anymore. They took it from him.

Today's Red Sox

A reporter asked me if the Red Sox are better now, in terms of their image. I told him that John Henry and them are trying to clean it up. I don't think they want any of the old reputation anymore, but some of those old owners left a deep impression that's going to be difficult to cover over. It's hard to do. Changing a reputation is probably the hardest thing that anyone can do. I don't think changing that old-world reputation of the Red Sox as a racist organization is a concentrated-on thing every day, but I think it's important to them to change it.

The fans—both the white fans and the minorities—a lot of them don't even know. I mean, if you're not 80 years old you probably don't remember Pumpsie Green. You probably don't know anything about George Scott or Earl Wilson, either. The only modern-day ballplayers that most fans can probably relate to are Jimmy Rice, myself, Ellis Burks, Mike Easler, guys like that.

Drifting Apart

I wasn't at my own dad's funeral. He wasn't a dad to me. Maybe he was a dad to my older brothers, but not to me. I didn't have him my whole life—he left me when I was young. So I didn't see him like they saw him.

Peoples' dads leave them all the time. It depends on how they treat you when they leave—not that they left you. People break up all the goddamn time. I know that. I wasn't selfish, but it didn't help to have a fucked-up stepmom. So that kind of created more distance, too. Because I kind of judged him by the person that he replaced my mom with. He kind of threw his first family away when he got his second family. I didn't take that real good. Nothing could replace my mom, in no form or fashion. That's why I concentrate on being a really good daddy with my kids.

You're your mom's baby—your daddy's maybe. Remember that. You're definitely your momma's child, but you can be any other man's kid. I lost a lot of respect for him, and that's what I don't want to lose with my kids. So I concentrate on that a lot, because I want my babies to be at my funeral.

World Baseball Classic

You know what pissed me off about the World Baseball Classic? Why couldn't we put an all African American team in there? We were denied by Bud Selig. I'm the one who started it up. He didn't know that, but I'm the one who made CC Sabathia and all them go to Major League Baseball and ask, "Can we put an all African American team in the tournament?" And I told those black players, "I'm through with you motherfuckers if y'all play with the USA team.

"You're supposed to be out there representing Satchel Paige and Josh Gibson and Cool Papa Bell and the rest of the Negro League, because we're all descendants of them. You should be able to go in there and tell them that you want to put nine black men on the field in the World Baseball Classic. They got an All-Mexican team, an All-Cuban team, an All-Dominican team. They got an All-Venezuelan team and they even got a team from Italy. Why, when it came down to America's team, do they got blacks and whites playing on the same team?"

Why do they do that? That shows you that they don't want our mind thinking about where we came from. "Fuck the African

American ballplayer," is what they're saying. That's what they said. So don't go to talking to me about all these RBI programs and that kind of stuff. It don't mean a thing, because you got 100 schools down in the Dominican Republic—every team down there's got a camp, got a school. I went down there two years in a row to play winter ball, and they wouldn't even let me play winter ball, because the United States owns all the fucking teams down there. They pretty much own the whole damn island. The only thing that's down there besides baseball is some Africans walking around with food on their heads.

Everybody else is an ex-major leaguer or their kids or grand kids. Everybody on the island is a descendant of a ballplayer. Not one person down there isn't a cousin or a grandchild of somebody who played professional baseball. It's a place where they know you can go down there and pick ballplayers like they're apples, so what do they need with African Americans.

Steroids

Personally, I don't think that steroids enhanced ballplayers like they said it did. I mean, if you're a pitcher, it's not going to make you a better one because you throw harder. We've already said hard throwers get hit hard all over the field, so it doesn't have anything to do with being able to be a better pitcher.

Roger being so good at an advanced age? That's not so unusual to me. Him staying healthy is the key to that, because steroids don't make you healthy. Look at Nolan Ryan. He was never the pitcher that Roger was, as far as a *pitcher*. Nolan learned how to be a pitcher his last 10 years in the game. But Nolan was throwing the ball 96 mph at 45 years old down in Texas. You need a different type of mentality, an endurance mentally. Even if he did steroids, I don't really think it enhanced

Roger. What I think it did was make guys recover faster. I was a pitcher, and I can tell you there wasn't any time when I went out there where I felt 100 percent. I would always feel somewhere from 65 to 75 percent as far as physical.

You pitch every five days. It's a long season. Thirty-five starts. Throwing 110 pitches a ballgame 35 times. I think if you go out there and you start 35 ballgames, I think only 15 of them you feel good, 10 or so you get through it, the other ones you feel like shit. I think if you took steroids you probably felt good 25 of those games. It's not going to make you pitch better, but you're going to feel better, you're going to have more stamina. You're going to be able to go out there and probably throw those 100 pitches or so effortlessly, compared to if you weren't on them. We all know that pitchers go through a dead arm somewhere during the season. Somewhere, your velocity is going to drop a little bit. If you're throwing 95 it might drop to 88, 89, 90. It's just the natural fatigue in there. With a few days rest, doing what you have to do, the velocity can come and go.

But all that still won't make you hit spots, get balls where you have to, get people popping balls up, jamming people, getting people out.

I think it was maybe 10 percent of players that took PEDs when I was in the game. I could look at guys and tell that that's not a baseball physique, especially when they were very agile, very limber, and not muscle-bound. You could look at guys and tell it wasn't a natural body type. It was freakish, because if you were muscle-bound then you couldn't have a fluid arm or swing. But these guys had the same motion and everything, just bigger and stronger.

But if guys were body builders and gained all this weight from going to the gym, then they're not going to be as flexible. They're going to be tighter. They're not going to be limber. They can't even bend over and touch their toes. They can't even scratch their head because they're all bulked up. But these guys bulked up and they're flexible. That was the part that made it kind of freakish, like, "Damn, man."

You could tell Bo Jackson was a football player swinging a bat. You could see the unpolished technique of just swinging a bat very violently. He didn't go after the ball with a pretty swing, with a real technical swing that's compact and powerful. You could see a massive, strong-ass man whipping a bat. Bo never took a steroid in his life. But he looked like he did. He looked like a man who did weights and was tight and bulky. So, you see, sometimes you can't tell just by looking.

He looked like a football player. But lots of these guys were freakishly strong and fluid. Science might say differently, but you ain't hitting the ball that much farther just because of steroids. I don't know if Sammy Sosa ever took steroids. A lot of people think he did, but I'll tell you, he was already a slugger. There's no way taking steroids added 30 home runs. That was him.

Plus, there are other reasons for home runs increases. Everybody was saying in the late '80s and early '90s that the ball was juiced, remember.

Wade Boggs, for instance, hit all those home runs that one year and I looked at his ball card recently and the most he ever hit before that was like eight. But Wade couldn't be questioned for it because Wade wasn't tight and didn't get muscles and things. He just had really big calves and big forearms and strong hands. I think that Wade was just strong. He was a contact guy like Rod Carew or Tony Gwynn, just a lot stronger. It enabled him to hit balls harder than a lot of guys. He even hit the ball real hard on the ground. Like Fred Lynn said, "Nobody hit the ball harder on the ground than Wade. Nobody."

Are you saying Dustin Pedroia's juiced because he hits 20 balls out of the park? Some people who don't know anything just assume guys like Dustin are juiced. He's one of the smallest men in the big leagues and he's hitting the ball like that? Come on. But the truth is, he's not juicing. He's stronger than hell and he has bat speed and hand strength. That's where it comes from. Ian Kinsler's the same way.

A reporter once asked me why I didn't use steroids. The answer is simple: I didn't know about them. And I don't think I would have anyway because I've always wanted to be a guy that beat you on skill and out-thinking you. I always thought that was the best way to be an athlete: I beat you to the punch. I anticipated you doing something so I was able to counteract that. I had that mentality, though I've often thought that it was missing in the major leagues. Some people even told me that if I gained 20 pounds I could throw harder. Wade Boggs told me that. He's the first person who ever said that to me. And I didn't know what he was talking about. He thought that if I went home in the off-season and I beefed up and got bigger that I would throw harder.

Now that I'm older I think maybe he was talking about steroids. He never said that to me, but once I learned about this whole steroid thing I started thinking, maybe he meant I should juice up and get bigger. But even if it was, it was just advice. Wade didn't use them, believe that. He didn't have to. He was as strong as a caveman.

My Antics

I was very animated on the mound. I knew it was showman time. I knew, because that's the way I grew up playing baseball. My dad said to get approval of how good you are you have to make those people clap for you. That's what he told us growing up. That's how you knew if you were a good baseball player, if those people clapped for you. They boo you when you're doing bad and clap for you when you're doing good. When they boo you that means they love you, because that means that you should be doing better than you're doing. Getting booed is part of being a good ballplayer. That should wake your ass up.

I was an activist within myself. I wasn't trying to be anything; it was just the way my life led me to be that way. To be called "boy" growing up, to be called "nigger," or anything else demeaning, it became second nature to fight back at anything that I heard that was negative. It even became second nature to fight for others, when others wouldn't speak. My father-in-law said that to me. He said I may have got my ass kicked out of the game, but I did help change the game. I did a lot in the game to be able to give a black kid today a mind to speak a little bit.

Barnstormin'

In '07, Delino DeShields and I attempted to bring baseball down to Mississippi. We were trying to get the African American fan back to the game of baseball. The way things have gone with black kids not playing the game, it's almost like we're going back to the beginning, when there were no blacks in the game. Baseball had its own fan base, but blacks weren't playing the game.

What we were trying to do with this barnstormin' thing was to get back to the old fun persona of the game. We were trying to get to different towns around the country with some ex-major and minor leaguers and a few Dominican ballplayers. We called it "Oil Can Boyd and the Traveling All-Stars," after "Bingo Long and the Traveling All-Stars." It featured me, Delino DeShields, Wendell Magee, and others. We only had three or four ex-major league ballplayers on the team, but we had very good ballplayers.

We went to Canada. We went to Montgomery, Alabama. We went to Pittsfield and Brockton, Massachusetts, and Nashua, New Hampshire. I scheduled some exhibition games with some independent teams before the season started. The weather didn't permit us to do that much—the game in Brockton basically got flooded out because of the time of the year. If we could have done it in the South it would have been better. That would have allowed us to receive more of a black audience.

We didn't really do it to make money. We did it to try and create an attitude and bring back black people's passion for the game of baseball. And if they saw Delino DeShields and myself and other guys attempting to do that then things would have grown from there. We were hoping to get in touch with different black coaches, different colleges, and things like that so that we would be able to come to different places and maybe play some exhibition ballgames. We could've played some semi-pro games in those Southern cities against existing teams, just like we did in Montgomery. And if we could have barnstormed down through Louisiana and different places, we probably could have played 100 ballgames.

But we did it back East. It was real good. It lasted for just two weeks or so, but it was something that got us attention and it got me out there doing what I love to do. What I wanted to do eventually was to try to one day put together some type of really good black traveling team to go to the Caribbean, South America, Panama, and different countries—almost like the Harlem Globetrotters. Everybody knows who the Harlem Globetrotters are, but the thing everybody knows first and foremost about the Harlem Globetrotters is that they're black.

The entertainment comes second. Their razzle-dazzle and their uniforms and the whole global thing came later. First it started out as some black athletes. That's what caught the attention of people all around the world. We thought that if the kids saw a black traveling baseball team it could really teach them to love the game. We thought it could be just like the Indianapolis Clowns back in the '30s, '40s, and early '50s, traveling around and barnstormin' like the King and his Court traveling softball team.

We wanted to get the attention of blacks in the country who could start focusing on, "Oh, okay, we heard about this, we didn't know about this Negro League thing." Then you get into these towns and what you're doing is attracting and teaching the younger kids who love the game of baseball. They can shake the hands of some ex-major leaguers, some ex-pro ballplayers, some guys who love the game and love the kids. Then we'd stay for a little bit and meet folks and run a clinic and things like that.

You have to go and get the people. They're not going to come to you unless you go and get them. This is the best way to get blacks back into the game of baseball. People don't understand what this meant to my race at one period of time in this country. But I do care about my people and I do understand that my people in this country are descendants of indentured servants or slaves. It's one or the other.

Believe me, the people in the South know about the Negro Leagues. They know it very well. We still have black baseball played in the South—semi-pro baseball that I play now that goes back to when I was a child. We still have all-black baseball in little towns all over Alabama, Mississippi, Tennessee, Georgia, and parts of Florida.

In the South, you still have the old-timers—70 to 90 years old—who come out to the ballgames. They still come out to the sandlot ballgames out in the country, in the cow pastures.

The people there know these guys were ballplayers, and the old ballplayers and fans are still talking about Satchel Paige and Josh Gibson, and they make sure in the South that you'll never forget that Willie Mays played with the Birmingham Barons—and they'll never, ever forget that in Birmingham. They'll never forget that Hank Aaron is from Mobile, Alabama. It's always going to be in the South where we know of Satchel Paige and that'll never leave Mobile, or Hattiesburg, Mississippi. He was born in Mobile but lived the second part of his life in Hattiesburg.

We played the Olympic Team in Pittsfield, Massachusetts. Dan Duquette set that up. Joba Chamberlain was on that team. He started the game against us, but we didn't know who he was at the time. We only knew that this kid was throwing harder than hell. He was what, 19? 20? Maybe 21? I mean, this kid was throwing hard—everybody out there, all these young kids, I don't know where they all are now, but I imagine that some of them have to be in the major leagues.

We didn't know who they were, but they were very good ballplayers. They beat us 7–1. I came in the ballgame and threw a couple innings and pitched well. We pitched some kids who I had that were wild on the mound, so it gave them the opportunity to run the bases and do some things.

Delino swung the bat well—all our guys swung the bat well—and "Bop" hadn't hit in five years. His legs weren't like they would normally be, but he made nice plays, including a delayed steal at 37 years old when hadn't played in a while. That lets you know what kind of athlete he is.

But we got a chance to play flamboyantly. We got a chance to play as though we were Negro Leaguers. Our style of play wasn't showboating, it was just enjoyment. It was no different than on an NBA basketball court today. That's what we did. That's the way we played baseball. We talked on the field—we called it "jenkin" and those guys called it trash talking. We created that on the basketball court. Trash talking? Naw. We were just talking about yo' mama while we were having fun.

Teaching the Game

I teach baseball. When I give these little seminars the parents always compliment me on how blessed I am to be able to put the science with the talent. That's when I tell them that it doesn't take as much natural talent as they've been told. A 76 mph fastball is the same as a 96 mph fastball. This always confuses them. So then I explain that if you threw a 76 mph fastball up to the plate and then you threw a 51 mph change-up, you're going to get the same results as a man following a 96 mph fastball with an 85 mph change-up. The ball is going to look the same. That's the part of the game they don't understand, and that's why you shouldn't put radar guns on kids. You should teach them how to pitch and they'll pitch a long time. And the game will be played with more skill and more ingenuity. If they would let guys with brains go out and hit spots as opposed to going 3–2 to everybody, the game would be better for it.

I like to see a guy go out and bust a fastball in on your hands, and when you swing you hit it foul. Then he throws you a straight change-up at your knees and you roll it over and hit it at the third baseman. And the next time you're up he comes back and does the same, just the opposite. He throws you a straight change-up on the first pitch, away, and you roll it over to third again, or you pop it up.

The guys today don't understand that. I pitched in a ballgame once in Montreal, and for five straight innings I threw a straight change-up every pitch. I did it just to see what it would do, because I had great command of it and I knew the science of what a change-up is. I didn't use it as a show-me pitch. As a matter of fact, it was my most-definite out pitch, and I would sometimes throw it to a batter three times in a row. Three times in a row in three at-bats in a row. He would see nine change-ups. If he didn't swing and pop up the first one, well I'm still trying to get him to pop up the second one, without diverting to another pitch.

I was able to change speeds and hit locations, so it wasn't ever the same pitch twice. Clay Buchholz, for instance, has a really good change-up, but it could be a great change-up if he spotted it. It's not enough to just throw a good one, you have to be able to spot it like you do a fastball.

That's the deception. As a pitcher, I have to know that if I throw a straight change-up to you, down and away, to a lefty or a righty, the ball looks like a fastball—100 percent like a fastball—and you're going to swing out front. The only time you should be able get the good part of the bat on it is if I leave it in a little bit. Smart hitters can kind of get a feel for you, and they'll try to set you up and wait on that pitch. But if you got the good arm speed, and you locate it, then they're in for a long game.

That's why I tell people that the pitching coaches are not teaching pitching. I mean, take a look at who the pitching coaches are. You ever notice that Greg Maddux and Tom Glavine are not pitching coaches? These guys are 300-game winners. Don't you wonder why these guys are not brought in right away to be pitching coaches? You'd think that they would be, but what they knew how to do is hard to teach to this class of pitchers that they got throwing 97 and 98 all night.

A pitcher can't just be taught to do the things that I know how to do. I used to start out already knowing what I was going to throw the next guy—not the guy on deck, the guy in the hole. I've already pitched to all three of them in my mind. How do I do that? With control. With control I could plan ahead, because I knew I wasn't going to miss where I threw the baseball.

Today's Baseball Player

Today's baseball player is a better athlete than the players were when I played. Today's baseball player is a better all-around player, I guess, because the teaching of the game is a little bit more intense than it was. The game has evolved quite a bit and the athlete has evolved. The technology that's in the game—the video and the statistical data and all that stuff—it's changed the game quite a bit. Now a ballplayer can study the game of baseball more so than the ballplayer of the past could. Hitters can study the pitcher. The pitcher can study the hitter.

It's not just the ballplayer; the game has changed too. Now the officiating has a lot to do with the way the game is played. For instance, the fact that the pitcher can't consistently throw the ball with malice inside. You can't use that inside fastball as a waste pitch or a purpose pitch like it was when I was playing. When you had a batter 0-and-2, nine times out of 10 the next pitch or the next two pitches were coming inside. Today, I see quite a bit of that has changed, where the pitcher is using the outer half of the plate instead of the inner half of the plate to get hitters out. Maybe that's been dictated by safety measures in the game or whatever.

Now you see batting averages going up because the hitters are more comfortable at the plate and you see ERAs going up because the pitcher can't protect the inside of the plate like he used to. And when you can't consistently pitch inside then you're going to have to try to get a major league hitter out by pitching over the plate and that's hard to do. So it has driven up the batting averages, the RBIs, all the offensive parts of the game. It has changed tremendously. Defense is never going to change—you have to catch it, you have to throw it.

The baseball player today is more mentally prepared to go out and play the game because of the way game has been analyzed and how mental the game has become. We've always known it was a mental game, but the day has really come where the emphasis is really on it. But a lot of players can't think like that, and that's when you see the game not being executed like it should be. Lots of pitchers haven't gotten with the program as far as being able to locate the ball consistently, hit their spots, understand what it means to out-think a hitter. Those are the guys you see having a hard time in the game. Those are the mediocre ballplayers. That's where you take a major leaguer and he becomes mediocre. That's where you see a guy in the major leagues who's 12–12 with a five-point-something ERA.

A lot of that is also because of the fact that today's scouts are told to go out and look for strong arms and the game has gone to the radar gun. If a kid's not throwing 95 he's suspect. It used to be 90, but now they're looking for a kid who can consistently throw the fastball in the mid- to upper 90s. The average fastball is not 88 anymore. The average fastball in the major leagues right now is 92. So that's why the pitch counts are going up, because they're not teaching the young kids how to pitch. They're teaching the young kids about velocity and throwing hard. That's not teaching them how to persevere in the game. That's not going to create longevity—that's going to create injuries. And that's why you see a lot of young kids right now having arm problems. Their arms are more stressed because their fastball is maxing out at a certain velocity, and all these young kids are thinking, "Man, I have to throw harder, I have to throw harder." That's where the emphasis is. Instead of pitching to contact, a kid is pitching to swings and misses. When you're a pitcher who pitches to contact, the games are going to move faster.

You've got time limits (between pitches) in a Major League Baseball game, which I've always thought should never exist. But when you've got kids out there throwing 100 pitches in five innings you need them. I've never heard of anything like that but that's because of the hard thrower. And every smart pitcher knows that the harder you throw, the more pitches you're going to have fouled off. So there should be more emphasis on telling pitchers to go out and pitch to contact and location and try to perplex the batter, instead of brute strength and going right at hitters. The people who're teaching baseball to kids need to stop saying, "Go as hard as you can for as long as you can." That's not the mentality that you want to give a kid when you're talking about trying to pitch 10 to 15 years in the major leagues.

The game has changed quite a bit in that sense, to where I see that everybody in the major leagues right now has hard throwers. Everybody is running a guy out there who's throwing 96 or 97, guys who've had Tommy John surgery, too. And the breaking ball is not being properly taught. I can look at someone like Kerry Wood or this new kid, Strasburg, and see that down the road they're going to have surgery. In both of them I saw that, and both of them had surgery. When I can see and tell when you're going to throw a breaking ball by your delivery, that tells me that you're going to have a problem with your arm. When I can see the grip on your hand and the tension in your elbow and in your forearm, that means that you're not gripping the ball properly to throw that breaking ball and you're going to end up hurting your ulnar nerve.

I know about that. I went through that and I changed the way I threw the baseball, so I never had that problem ever again in my elbow. It had been because of the way I was gripping the ball and throwing the breaking ball. There are a lot of pitching coaches in the major leagues right now who I can't comprehend what they're telling these kids. I don't want to say that they don't know what they're doing, I just feel that it's their job that these kids learn to pitch to contact. It can't be talking so much about how they feel—*Is it a good day or a bad day, etc.*—I'd say that out of the 200 or so games that I started in the major leagues, I'd like to think that I felt good in only about a third of them. You have to be able to go out there and get people out when you don't feel great, when your stuff isn't there. That's pitching, when you put emphasis on how to get people out. I really think that from what I'm seeing today, not enough young kids go out there and become the type of pitcher that a Roy Halladay is. I'm not seeing that.

I'm not even seeing that from the aces on staffs. Roy is even above the aces on other peoples' staffs in that he pitches to contact. And that's why he's out there completing ballgames, and he's completing ballgames at 100 pitches. That's outstanding, and that's the way I was completing ballgames. It's so different.

The batter is stronger today. There's more emphasis on bat speed. The bats themselves have changed. They're harder because of the type of wood they're using. Also, now the bats are made perfect for the batter, the weight, the balance, everything. Even the baseball itself is harder. The ballparks have shrunk. There used to be bigger ballparks when I was playing. Now there are smaller ballparks and that's for the offense, so today's pitcher is catching a hard time in the major leagues.

It's an offensive game today, more so than it was when I was playing. It was more of a defensive game then. We didn't have shortstops who hit 30 home runs when I played. Shortstops and second basemen are hitting 30 home runs today. When I played, my second baseman and shortstop might have hit 15 together. But they played superb defense and beautiful, smart baseball. Overall, the offensive numbers weren't up like they are now. Lots of teams have five or six guys in the lineup with 100 RBIs. That was unheard of. You only used to have that from the third, fourth, and fifth hitters when I was playing. You're getting that kind of production out of guys batting eighth. You have a year like '11, for instance. Jacoby Ellsbury hit 32 bombs and drove in more than 100 runs from the leadoff spot. Has anyone ever done that? I don't think anybody has ever done that. And that shows you right there that the game has changed, when a leadoff hitter gets over 100 RBIs. That shows you how potent the offense is, but it also shows you how poor the pitching is.

You know, I heard someone talking recently about Roger Maris, the game itself, steroid eras, all those types of things. They were trying to compare the eras, and let me tell you, you just can't. That's when you know you're not talking to a ballplayer, because you can analyze the numbers and read records all you want, but a ballplayer can tell you that baseball in the '60s was not like baseball today. Baseball in the '50s was not like baseball today. Baseball didn't start being like the game it is today until the '70s. My father-in-law and I were talking about it and I said, "If you're going to put asterisks by people's names, put it by Babe Ruth's name, put it by Ted Williams' name, put it by every ballplayer who played from '65 back. Put it by their names." Jackie Robinson may have integrated baseball in '47, but it wasn't until the mid-'60s that the league was fully integrated. So from '65 back everything should have an asterisk next to it. You didn't play against Satchel Paige, Ted Williams, because you wouldn't have hit shit. Satchel wasn't going to stand out there and let you hit his ball like that without knocking your ass down every other pitch. You want to put asterisks by names, you have to put asterisks by all of those guys who didn't have to play against black ballplayers.

Back in the day, when Jackie signed, the game wasn't the same. And when the African Americans—and African-descendant ballplayers like the Dominicans and Puerto Ricans, etc.—started coming into the game it put life and color into the game. But now the African American player is expendable. This country ain't no island like the Dominican Republic or some little country like Venezuela. This country ain't South America and it ain't Central America. This is America. This country's run differently, so the African American ballplayer is expendable, because baseball can go to the Dominican Republic right now and get some guy who looks just like Oil Can Boyd and bring him over. They don't have to even worry about paying him the kind of money that an African American would ask for in the draft. Because whatever else people may think about African Americans they're still Americans, and they know their rights and their value.

That was part of the stigma they put on me. There are all kind of different black ballplayers in the game with personalities and attitude. I'm just the only one they considered "pro black." They had all kinds of blacks they considered "right," who followed their rules. But they knew that they could come to me and say, "Dennis, we're going to give you a $10 million contract if you just quiet it down a little bit," and I wasn't going to take that contract. They knew I couldn't be bought. They knew that they couldn't change my personality or the type of person that I was.

That was an insult to them, because they felt that they could change every black man if they give them money. They already knew that they didn't have to worry about the white kids, because two-thirds of the white ballplayers came from silver spoons. They already knew that they came from good family backgrounds. They didn't come from trailer parks and projects. Two-thirds of Major League Baseball players were well-to-do white kids way before they ever threw a baseball in the major leagues. As country as a guy like John Lackey seems, I bet his family probably owned a ranch growing up. Back-wooded as you may think a white person is, it probably wasn't so bad. I grew up in the South. I know poor whites. I know there are cases that are different, but I still say today: a white kid who is growing up in a single-family home is still better off than a black kid growing up in a single-family home. No question about it.

I'm going to tell you, if it wasn't for the African-descendant ballplayer I don't know where baseball would be today. And that's the Dominican, the Puerto Rican, the Venezuelan, the Nicaraguan, all players of color. You wouldn't have the game that you have today. That's why right now, whites are finding it harder and harder to look at TV and lie to themselves. They used to look at Big Papi and say he was different than Oil Can but they don't do that today. The Dominican won't allow you to do that today. They used to say to us that they were different. Now how are you different than me? Where are you different than me at? Explain that to me. That's what I used to say to the Dominicans and Puerto Ricans in the minor leagues. Your language? Please. Matter of fact, you're *more* African than me. I'm in America, motherfucker. I'm watered down. I'm three people—I'm Irish and Indian and African. Your ass is just African! Big Papi? That's an African—way more than I am.

A fan doesn't look at the game and see Pedro Martinez as a Dominican or a Latino. They see a black man pitching. So now, when they go on talking about how there aren't any African Americans in the game I tell them they're mistaken. I've had this argument with Delino, with Torii Hunter and CC, and I tell them all the same thing.

You look at the game today and even though the number of African Americans is going down, the game is still 75 percent black! The game is still black people and white people and a few Asians mixed in. But the game is mostly black and white. It ain't Latin, African American, and white. What you mean to tell me, you don't have Italians on the field? You don't have any Norwegians or Irish or Germans on the field? On the field, they're all considered what? White. They're not out there talking about Mike Piazza and Dustin Pedroia and Roger Clemens and them as being different, are they?

When I say Big Papi is black, I mean he's African. He's black. If you're black then you're African. It's just like Bob Marley said, "If you a black man, you an Afri-can." So I don't give a damn what language you speak, because there ain't one of us in this country whose name is goddamn Kin-tay. Not one of us. All our names, like Johnson and Jones and Smith, at the core they're just the same as Pujols and Martinez and Ortiz.

Statistics

Dennis "Oil Can" Boyd

Born: 10/06/1959 (Meridian, Mississippi)
Bats: Right
Throws: Right
Height: 6'1"
Weight: 155 pounds
Drafted: 1980—16th Round (414 overall)

Pitching Stats

Year	Team	G	GS	W	L	ERA	CG	SHO	IP	H	ER	R	BB	SO
1982	Red Sox	3	1	0	1	5.40	0	0	8.1	11	5	5	2	2
1983	Red Sox	15	13	4	8	3.28	5	0	98.2	103	36	46	23	43
1984	Red Sox	29	26	12	12	4.37	10	3	197.2	207	96	109	53	134
1985	Red Sox	35	35	15	13	3.70	13	3	272.1	273	112	117	67	154
1986	Red Sox	30	30	16	10	3.78	10	0	214.1	222	90	99	45	129
1987	Red Sox	7	7	1	3	5.89	0	0	36.2	47	24	31	9	12
1988	Red Sox	23	23	9	7	5.34	1	0	129.2	147	77	82	41	71
1989	Red Sox	10	10	3	2	4.42	0	0	59	57	29	31	19	26
1990	Expos	31	31	10	6	2.93	3	3	190.2	164	62	64	52	113
1991	Expos	19	19	6	8	3.52	1	1	120.1	115	47	49	40	82
1991	Rangers	12	12	2	7	6.68	0	0	62	81	46	47	17	33
Career 10 Years		**214**	**207**	**78**	**77**	**4.04**	**43**	**10**	**1,389.20**	**1,427**	**624**	**680**	**368**	**799**

Fielding Stats

Year	Team	POS	G	TC	TC/G	PO	A	E	DP	FLD%
1982	Red Sox	P	3	1	0.3	0	1	0	0	1
1983	Red Sox	P	15	16	1.1	5	10	1	1	0.938
1984	Red Sox	P	29	53	1.8	20	31	2	3	0.962
1985	Red Sox	P	35	84	2.4	42	41	1	2	0.988
1986	Red Sox	P	30	53	1.8	24	27	2	4	0.962
1987	Red Sox	P	7	15	2.1	4	11	0	0	1
1988	Red Sox	P	23	25	1.1	8	15	2	0	0.92
1989	Red Sox	P	10	17	1.7	7	10	0	1	1
1990	Expos	P	31	34	1.1	7	24	3	1	0.912
1991	Expos	P	19	18	0.9	7	11	0	0	1
1991	Rangers	P	12	10	0.8	4	6	0	1	1
Career 10 Years		**P**	**214**	**326**	**1.5**	**128**	**187**	**11**	**13**	**0.96**

About the Authors

Dennis "Oil Can" Boyd

Dennis "Oil Can" Boyd rose from the poverty and racism of 1960s Mississippi to become one of the most colorful and memorable players in Major League Baseball history. Boyd played for the Boston Red Sox, Montreal Expos, and Texas Rangers during his 10-year career, including a 16-win season for the unforgettable 1986 Red Sox. He currently lives in East Providence, Rhode Island.

Mike Shalin

Mike Shalin is a 35-year sports journalism veteran. The 1976 graduate of Wichita State University started with the wire services in New York in the 1970s, moved to the *New York Post* from 1980–82, and then spent 22 years at the *Boston Herald*, covering the Red Sox for 12 years and then Boston College football and basketball before leaving the newspaper in 2005. A Baseball Hall of Fame voter since 1989, Shalin is now a freelancer in the Boston area whose varied duties include working as an official scorer at Fenway Park. He is the author of *Donnie Baseball*, and the co-author of *Out by a Step, The 100 Best Players Not in the Baseball Hall of Fame* and *Gilles Villemure's Tales from the Rangers Locker Room*. He has authored several books for young readers. Shalin resides in Easton, Massachusetts.